Series/Number 07-104

# MULTIPLE ATTRIBUTE DECISION MAKING
## An Introduction

**K. PAUL YOON**
*Fairleigh Dickinson University*

**CHING-LAI HWANG**
*Kansas State University*

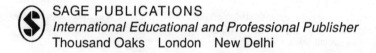

SAGE PUBLICATIONS
*International Educational and Professional Publisher*
Thousand Oaks   London   New Delhi

*For information address:*

SAGE Publications, Inc.
2455 Teller Road
Thousand Oaks, California 91320

SAGE Publications Ltd.
6 Bonhill Street
London EC2A 4PU
United Kingdom

SAGE Publications India Pvt. Ltd.
M-32 Market
Greater Kailash I
New Delhi 110 048 India

Printed in the United States of America

**Library of Congress Cataloging-in-Publication Data**

Yoon, Kwangsun, 1947-
    Multiple attribute decision making: an introduction / K. Paul
Yoon, Ching-Lai Hwang
        p.   cm. — (Sage university papers series. Quantitative
applications in the social sciences; no. 07-104)
    Includes bibliographical references.
    ISBN 0-8039-5486-7
    1. Decision-making—Mathematical models.   I. Hwang, C. L. (Ching
-Lai), 1929-  II. Title.  III. Series.
HD30.23.Y66  1995
658.4′ 03—dc20                                               94-45234

95  96  97  98  99  10  9  8  7  6  5  4  3  2  1

Sage Project Editor: Susan McElroy

When citing a university paper, please use the proper form. Remember to cite the current Sage University Paper series title and include the paper number. One of the following formats can be adapted (depending on the style manual used):

(1) YOON, K. P., and HWANG, C.-L. (1995) *Multiple Attribute Decision Making: An Introduction.* Sage University Paper series on Quantitative Applications in the Social Sciences, 07-104. Thousand Oaks, CA: Sage.

OR

(2) Yoon, K. P., & Hwang, C.-L. (1995) *Multiple attribute decision making: An introduction* (Sage University Paper series on Quantitative Applications in the Social Sciences, 07-104). Thousand Oaks, CA: Sage.

# CONTENTS

# SERIES EDITOR'S INTRODUCTION

It can be quite difficult for decision makers to make the "best" choice, try as they might. In selecting among alternatives, they must juggle many, sometimes contradictory, goals. They might do well to turn to Multiple Attribute Decision Making (MADM) methods. Formally defined by our authors, MADM means "making preference decisions (e.g., evaluation, prioritization, selection) over the available alternatives that are characterized by multiple, usually conflicting, attributes." MADM methodology is rigorous but normative, aimed at improving decision quality. As Drs. Yoon and Hwang felicitously report, Benjamin Franklin referred to his own version as "moral or prudential algebra."

MADM procedures can be applied to a wide range of human choices, from the professional to the managerial to the political. To take a professional example, suppose Barbara White, newly awarded her Ph.D., must decide which job to accept: Alternative 1, a tenure-track faculty position at a Big Ten university; Alternative 2, a postdoctoral fellowship in her speciality at an East Coast university; or Alternative 3, a research appointment with the Social Security Administration in Washington, D.C. In making her selection, Dr. White has to weigh the following attributes, or goals: Attribute 1, good salary; Attribute 2, professional satisfaction; and Attribute 3, geographic proximity to family. The decision is hard because each alternative promises to maximize a different attribute; for example, for Attribute 1, a good salary, she should select Alternative 3, the job with Social Security; but for Attribute 2, on professional satisfaction, she would prefer Alternative 2, the postdoc. How to decide?

There are numerous MADM methods, of which the authors have identified 13. Drawing on diverse disciplines, they illustrate them with many meaty examples, such as site selection for a waste management plant, a budget reduction decision, business manager selection, plant location, graduate school admission, and an automobile purchase. Chapter 3 begins in earnest with a discussion of "noncompensatory methods," that is, those for which a trade-off of attributes is not allowed. For example, to pursue our above example of selecting a job, the alternative that offered the highest salary would not be devalued if it also meant little professional satisfaction and a lack of geographic proximity to family.

Besides the several noncompensatory methods and scoring methods, the authors present the advanced procedures of TOPSIS and ELECTRE, the last of which has heavy French use. In a closing section there is a nice treatment of the Analytic Hierarchy Process (AHP), which may help the decision maker set up a hierarchy of attributes. They go over an intriguing application of AHP to President Carter's decision to try to rescue the American hostages in Iran. This monograph, with its focus on the systematic improvement of normative decisions, nicely complements the other decision making-related monographs of the series, such as *Multiattribute Evaluation* (No. 26, Edwards & Newman), *Introduction to Linear Goal Programming* (No. 56, Ignizio), *Linear Programming* (No. 60, Feiring), and *Analyzing Decision Making: Metric Conjoint Analysis* (No. 67, Louviere).

—*Michael S. Lewis-Beck*
Series Editor

# ACKNOWLEDGMENTS

A number of colleagues generously gave of their time to comment on an earlier version of this monograph. We would like to thank Shu-Jen Chen, Daniel Giordano, Young-Jou Lai, Robert J. Stawicki, and two anonymous reviewers. Our special thanks go to Shankar Raina, whose suggestions and graphic work made the monograph more comprehensible.

We wish to express our gratitude to the following institutions for the kind permission to adapt or reprint some materials from their publications: Decision Sciences Institute, which is located at Georgia State University, for Saaty, Vargas, and Barzilay (1982); Taylor and Frances, Ltd., for Yoon and Hwang (1985); US Ecology/Bechtel, Inc., for Paton and Bradbury (1987); and Pergamon Press, Ltd., for Swenson and McCahon (1991).

# MULTIPLE ATTRIBUTE DECISION MAKING
## An Introduction

**K. PAUL YOON**
*Fairleigh Dickinson University*

**CHING-LAI HWANG**
*Kansas State University*

## 1. INTRODUCTION

### 1.1. Multiple Attribute Decision Making

Decision makers (DMs) often deal with problems that involve multiple, usually conflicting, criteria. These problems may range from those affecting common households, such as the purchase of a car, to those affecting entire nations, as in the judicious use of dollars for the preservation of national security. For example, in purchasing a family car, the following multiple attributes may be considered: price, comfort (roominess), fuel economy, safety, maintenance cost, depreciation, appeal, and so on. The job one chooses may depend upon its prestige, location, salary, advancement opportunities, working conditions, and so on.

Each year about 1,500 out of 6,500 majors in the U.S. Army are selected for promotion to lieutenant colonel. Six criteria are used: military education level, civil education level, physical readiness and military bearing, officer qualifications, duty performance, and officer potential.

In its annual edition of "America's Best Colleges," *U.S. News & World Report* ranks academic institutions based on six attributes: academic reputation, student selectivity, faculty resources, financial resources, graduation rate, and alumni satisfaction.

National security is on the line when a DM must prioritize hundreds of critical items needed by the military. Suppose that an annual budget has been allocated for these critical military items whose total cost is more than double the allocation. Therefore, only the most important half of these items will get funded. In this instance, prioritization could be based on such criteria as readiness, sustainability, ease of supply, contribution to operations plans, and cost.

Multiple Attribute Decision Making (MADM) refers to making preference decisions (e.g., evaluation, prioritization, selection) over the available alternatives that are characterized by multiple, usually conflicting, attributes (Hwang & Yoon, 1981). MADM is a branch of the field of Multiple Criteria Decision Making (MCDM). MCDM also includes Multiple Objective Decision Making (MODM) (Hwang & Masud, 1979). In contrast to MADM problems, MODM problems involve designing the best alternative given a set of conflicting objectives. For example, automobile manufacturers wish to design a car that maximizes riding comfort and fuel economy and minimizes production cost. The alternatives are created by the design process, and their number can be as many as it produces.

The problems of MADM are diverse. However, even with the diversity, all the problems that are considered here share the following common characteristics:

*Alternatives:* A finite number of alternatives, from several to thousands, are screened, prioritized, selected, and/or ranked. For example, the number of alternative assembly plant sites in the United States a foreign automaker can select from may be less than ten, whereas an elite college may consider thousands of applicants for admission each year. The term "alternative" is synonymous with "option," "policy," "action," or "candidate," among others.

*Multiple Attributes:* Each problem has multiple attributes. A DM must generate relevant attributes for each problem setting. The number of attributes depends on the nature of the problem. For example, one may use price, gas mileage, safety, warranty period, workmanship, and style to evaluate cars; whereas there may be more than 100 factors to be considered in selecting a site for an auto assembly plant. The term "attributes" may be referred to as "goals" or "criteria."

*Incommensurable Units:* Each attribute has different units of measurement. In the car selection problem, gas mileage is expressed in miles per gallon, ride comfort in cubic feet (if measured by passenger space), and selling price in dollars, but safety is expressed in a nonnumerical way.

*Attribute Weights:* Almost all MADM methods require information regarding the relative importance of each attribute, which is usually supplied by an ordinal or cardinal scale. Weights can be assigned directly by the DM or may be developed by methods that are described in Section 2.2.

*Decision Matrix:* A MADM problem can be concisely expressed in a matrix format, where columns indicate attributes considered in a given problem and rows list competing alternatives. Thus a typical element $x_{ij}$ of the matrix indicates the performance rating of the $i$th alternative, $A_i$, with respect to the $j$th attribute, $X_j$.

## 1.2. Budget Reduction Decision: A MADM Case

In 1988, a significant budget reduction at the University of Wyoming left the Athletic Department nearly $700,000 short on operating funds compared to the previous biennium. The alternatives capable of realizing the proposed budget cuts included dropping an entire sport from the university's intercollegiate athletic family. After much deliberation only three feasible alternatives were presented: The elimination of $(A_1)$ the men's and women's ski programs, $(A_2)$ the baseball program, and $(A_3)$ the women's golf team. The Athletic Department decided on the following attributes to evaluate the alternatives: $(X_1)$ the number of people directly affected, $(X_2)$ money saved by the Athletic Department, and $(X_3)$ miscellaneous.

For the attribute of "people directly affected" the alternative values were calculated by adding the number of participants and coaches. The alternative values for the attribute of "money saved" represent only the funds saved in the first year after the sport was dropped. The "miscellaneous" attribute considered the indigenous factors (i.e., how "natural" it was to have the sport in the state), facility proximity, fan support, past success, and the facility required to maintain each sport. This category utilized a five-point cost scale ranging from *very low* to *very high,* with *very low* being the best.

The decision matrix for the Athletic Department budget problem can be seen in Table 1.1 (Swenson & McCahon, 1991). The selection is no longer a trivial task because each alternative has strong attribute ratings: for attribute $X_1$, alternative $A_3$, which affects the minimum number of people, is the best choice; for attribute $X_2$, alternative $A_1$, which offers the maximum cost saving, is the best; for attribute $X_3$, alternative $A_3$, which has a very low impact, is the best. In addition, alternative $A_2$ has intermediate ratings on each attribute. This problem will be analyzed by the ELECTRE method in Chapter 6.

TABLE 1.1
Decision Matrix of Program Termination for Athletic Department

| Programs | Attributes $X_1$ | $X_2$ | $X_3$ |
|---|---|---|---|
| $A_1$ : Drop skiing | 30 | $174,140 | Average (3) |
| $A_2$ : Drop baseball | 29 | $74,683 | Low (4) |
| $A_3$ : Drop women's golf | 12 | $22,496 | Very Low (5) |

NOTE: $X_1$ = number of people directly affected, $X_2$ = Athletic Department money saved, $X_3$ = miscellaneous.
SOURCE: Reprinted from Swenson and McCahon (1991, p. 540), ©1991, with kind permission from Pergamon Press Ltd, Headington Hill Hall, Oxford OX3 0BW, UK.

## 1.3. Ben Franklin's Solution: Classic MADM Approach

A classic piece of advice on MADM was rendered by Benjamin Franklin in a letter written to his friend Joseph Priestly (MacCrimmon, 1973):

London, Sept 19, 1772

Dear Sir,

In the affair of so much importance to you, wherein you ask my advice, I cannot, for want of sufficient premises, advise you what to determine, but if you please I will tell you how. When those difficult cases occur, they are difficult, chiefly because while we have them under consideration, all the reasons pro and con are not present to the mind at the same time; but sometimes one set present themselves, and at other times another, the first being out of sight. Hence the various purposes or inclinations that alternatively prevail, and the uncertainty that perplexes us. To get over this, my way is to divide half a sheet of paper by a line into two columns; writing over the one Pro, and over the other Con. Then, during three or four days consideration, I put down under the different heads short hints of the different motives, that at different times occur to me, for or against the measure. When I have thus got them all together in one view, I endeavor to estimate their respective weights; and where I find two, one on each side, that seem equal, I strike them both out. If I find a reason pro equal to some two reasons con, I strike out the three. If I judge some two reasons con, equal to three reasons pro, I strike out the five; and thus proceeding I find at length where the balance lies; and if, after a day or two of further consideration, nothing new that is of importance occurs on either side, I come to a determination accordingly. And, though the weight of the reasons cannot be taken with the precision of algebraic quantities, yet when each is thus considered, separately and comparatively, and the whole lies before me, I think I can judge better, and am less liable to make a rash step, and in fact I have found great advantage from this kind of equation, and what might be called moral or prudential algebra.

Wishing sincerely that you may determine for the best, I am ever, my dear friend, yours most affectionately.

B. Franklin

It is surprising to find that over 200 years ago Ben Franklin recognized the presence of multiple attributes in everyday decisions and suggested a workable solution. He perceived that each attribute has different weights and suggested appropriate trade-offs between conflicting attributes. Basically, Ben's advise was to list the pros and cons of alternatives and then cancel out one or more pros against one or more cons based on the respective weights assigned them by a DM. After following his advice a DM would be left with a fewer number of attributes, which should reduce the cognitive burden placed on him or her. Although Ben did not clearly mention how to pick the best(?) alternative, his technique is applicable to this day.

## 1.4. Classification of MADM Methods

MADM methods are management decision aids used in evaluating competing alternatives defined by multiple attributes. Ben Franklin's approach is a classic example. Pioneering surveys on MADM methods were carried out by MacCrimmon (1968, 1973). Since then many methods have been developed by researchers in disciplines as diverse as management science, economics, psychometrics, marketing research, applied statistics, and decision theory.

Hwang and Yoon (1981) classified a group of 17 MADM methods according to the type and salient features of information received from the DM. A modified taxonomy of 13 methods is shown in Figure 1.1. In this classification, methods are first categorized by the type of information received from the DM. If no information is given, the Dominance method is applicable. If information on the environment is given as either pessimistic or optimistic, the Maximin or Maximax method is applicable. If information on attributes is given, a subcategory, the salient feature of the information received from the DM, is used to further group the methods. The information given could be a standard (i.e., the minimum acceptable)

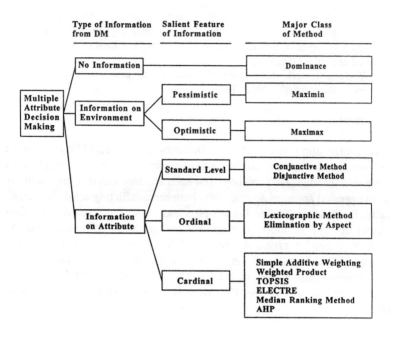

Figure 1.1. A Taxonomy of MADM Methods
SOURCE: Adapted from Hwang and Yoon (1981).

level of each attribute or may be attribute weights assessed by ordinal or cardinal scales.

## 1.5. Scope of the Monograph

Decision theories or methods have been categorized into normative or descriptive models depending on the way they are used. *Normative* models attempt to define the way a DM should make a decision. Hence, these models are designed to help people make optimal decisions. Practitioners of these types of models have their roots in management science, statistics, and economics. Associated with these models are an array of axioms and guiding principles that a rational DM should purportedly follow when making decisions (even those of a complex nature).

*Descriptive* models attempt to describe the way that DMs actually make decisions. These models are highly empirical and clinical in nature. Furthermore, many researchers have proven that DMs do not always make rational cognitive decisions and that they will systematically violate the axioms or principles set forth by normative models (Tversky & Kahneman, 1974, 1981). Proponents of these models have their backgrounds in the behavioral sciences, psychology, or marketing. Descriptive MADM models have been presented by Louviere (1988).

MADM models include not only models that describe human choice behavior but also models that specify methods for making optimal choices. Consider the following situations: A head of a household (male) buys a family car. His choice behavior may be forecasted by one of the descriptive models, which lies within the realm of behavioral science research. However, to rationalize his decision to the rest of the family he will have to use a normative model. When the Army wants to purchase a fleet of cars for a military function, it picks a normative model to select the cars that best meet its requirements. This model will naturally help the Army defend its choice over competing alternatives. Some MADM methods can be utilized for both descriptive and normative purposes. Hence, Bell, Raiffa, and Tversky (1988) referred to MADM models as *prescriptive* models.

The purpose of this monograph is to introduce the reader to normative MADM models. Some MADM methods in Chapter 3, which have been utilized for descriptive purposes, are included on the authors' belief that helping people make more nearly optimal decisions often requires that we understand how they currently make decisions. Hence, the reader should recognize that a MADM process outlined in Chapter 3 is only one of the many possible processes that a particular DM might use.

After a preparatory treatment including the generation of attributes in Chapter 2, efficient normative MADM methods coupled with various numerical examples are presented over five chapters. The examples are simple enough to be understandable, yet complex enough to illustrate the computational procedures and characteristics of each method. A number of real-world cases are also analyzed. The last chapter deals with the higher realms of MADM analysis, such as accommodation of soft data, construction of a multiple attribute decision support system, and the validity of methods.

# 2. ATTRIBUTE GENERATION, DATA, AND WEIGHT

MADM methodology tries to obtain a meaningful index from multidimensional data to evaluate competing alternatives. The analysis begins by establishing attributes that can measure relevant goal accomplishments. Alternatives are then contrasted over the chosen attributes. Often all attributes are not of equal importance to the DM. Consider, for example, the budget reduction problem illustrated in Table 1.1. The University of Wyoming identified nonmonetary attributes but did not give them as much importance as monetary attributes. Thus the rendering of appropriate weights among attributes is of prime concern to the DM.

Note that two of the attributes (people affected and money saved) in Table 1.1 were reported quantitatively, while the miscellaneous attribute was described qualitatively. Each quantitative attribute also has a different unit of measurement (number of people and dollars). Since most of the MADM methods require a homogenous data type, data transformation techniques become necessary. In this chapter we first present techniques for attribute generation and attribute weighting, then discuss the transformation and normalization of data in a decision matrix.

## 2.1. Attribute Generation

Multiple attribute decision analysis begins with the generation of attributes that should provide a means of evaluating goal accomplishments. Keeney and Raiffa (1976) suggest the use of a literature survey and/or a panel of experts to identify the attributes in the problem area. Although this may help enrich the set of attributes, it is necessary that the attributes represent the desired mission. One way of ensuring this is to derive the attributes hierarchically from a super goal. Goal hierarchy formulation starts with the listing of overall performance objectives serving a super goal. Pardee (1969) suggested that a desirable list of objectives (attributes) should:

1. *Be complete and exhaustive.* That is, all important performance attributes deemed relevant to the final decision should be represented by items on the list.

2. *Contain mutually exclusive items.* This would permit the DM to view listed attributes as independent entities among which appropriate trade-offs may later be made. This would also help prevent undesirable "double-counting" in the worth sense.

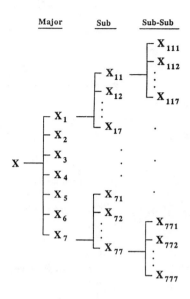

Figure 2.1. A Hierarchy Tree of Attributes
SOURCE: Chen and Hwang (1992).

3. *Be restricted to performance attributes of the highest degree of importance.* The purpose is to provide a sound basis or starting point from which lower-level criteria may subsequently be derived.

The goals at the top are usually quite abstract, such as "a good life," and become less so as one follows the hierarchy down. It is usually useful to go down the hierarchy until a measurable goal such as "family income" is reached. The lower level attributes should also be nonconflicting, coherent, and logical, as a set.

Figure 2.1 shows the generation of about 350 attributes using a hierarchial tree. Note that the major and sub attributes are all limited in number to seven. The number seven is based on Miller's theory (Miller, 1956) that seven plus or minus two represents the greatest amount of information that an observer can give us about an object on the basis of an absolute judgment.

A hierarchy of attributes for evaluating manufacturing plant sites is shown in Figure 2.2 to illustrate this process. It consists of four levels. First,

10

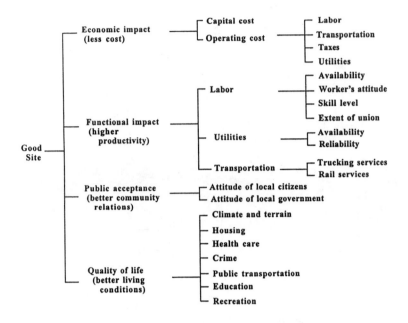

Figure 2.2. A Hierarchy of Attributes for Evaluating Plant Sites
SOURCE: Yoon and Hwang (1985).

four major attributes are identified that characterize a good site: less cost, higher productivity, better community relations, and better living conditions. Higher productivity, for instance, can be achieved by three subattributes: labor, utilities, and transportation. When a tangible attribute is not available yet, subdivisions are developed. For example, four sub-subattributes may measure the quality of "labor" reasonably well.

## 2.2. Attribute Weighting

As demonstrated in Ben Franklin's letter (Section 1.3), not all attributes are likely to be considered equally important. The role of weight serves to express the importance of each attribute relative to the others. Hence, the assignment of weights plays a key role in the MADM process and may vary from DM to DM. Weights should, of course, reflect the purpose of the evaluation. Moreover, the weights themselves are useful information to

TABLE 2.1
The 1992 Malcolm Baldrige Award
Examination Items and Point Values

| Categories (Attributes) | Point Value | (Weight) |
|---|---|---|
| 1.0  Leadership | 90 | (.09) |
| 2.0  Information and analysis | 80 | (.08) |
| 3.0  Strategic quality planning | 60 | (.06) |
| 4.0  Human resource development and management | 150 | (.15) |
| 5.0  Management of process quality | 140 | (.14) |
| 6.0  Quality and operational results | 180 | (.18) |
| 7.0  Customer focus and satisfaction | 300 | (.30) |
| Total | 1,000 | (1.00) |

those concerned with the program or project management, since they indicate what the DM is most concerned about in a quantitative way (Edwards & Newman, 1982). For example, in order to stimulate American companies to improve quality and productivity, the U.S. Department of Commerce established the Malcolm Baldrige National Quality Award. Table 2.1 shows the categories (i.e., attributes) for the award and their assigned weights. The weight on customer satisfaction is much higher than that of other categories, reflecting the Department's focus on the customer.

Many MADM methods require weight information from the DM. A DM may use either an ordinal or a cardinal scale to express his or her preference among attributes. Although it is usually easier for a DM to assign weights by an ordinal scale, most MADM methods require cardinal weights, that is, $w = (w_1, \ldots, w_j, \ldots, w_n)$ where $w_j$ is the weight assigned to the $j$th attribute. Cardinal weights are normalized to sum to 1, that is, $\sum w_j = 1$. There are numerous weight assessment techniques available. Good reviews can be found in Eckenrode (1965), Hobbs (1980), Hwang and Yoon (1981), and Voogd (1983).

### 2.2.1. Weights From Ranks

The simplest way of assessing weights is to arrange the attributes in a simple rank order, listing the most important attribute first and the least important attribute last. When we assign 1 to the most important attribute, and $n$ (the number of attributes at hand) to the least important, the cardinal weights can be obtained from one of the following formulas (Stillwell, Seaver, & Edwards, 1981):

$$w_j = \frac{\dfrac{1}{r_j}}{\displaystyle\sum_{k=1}^{n} \dfrac{1}{r_k}}$$

$$w_j = \frac{(n - r_j + 1)}{\displaystyle\sum_{k=1}^{n} (n - r_k + 1)}$$

where $r_j$ is the rank of the $j$th attribute. The weights obtained by the first formula are called rank reciprocal weights; and by the second formula, rank sum weights. If attributes are tied in the ranking, their mean ranking should be used. For instance, if two attributes are tied for the second and third place, the number 2.5 is assigned to both of them.

Ranking $n$ attributes at the same time may place a heavy cognitive burden on the DM. Therefore, a method by which a complete ranking can be obtained from a set of pairwise judgments is the preferred approach (Morris, 1964). This method requires the DM to make pairwise preference judgments between attributes. If there are $n$ attributes, a total of $n(n-1)/2$ comparisons (judgments) must be made. For example, assume that there are five attributes to be ranked, and the 10 pairwise judgments received from the DM are given as: $(X_1 > X_2)$, $(X_1 > X_3)$, $(X_1 > X_4)$, $(X_1 > X_5)$, $(X_2 < X_3)$, $(X_2 > X_4)$, $(X_2 < X_5)$, $(X_3 > X_4)$, $(X_3 < X_5)$, and $(X_4 < X_5)$, where the symbol ">" should be read as "is preferred to." This pairwise judgment data can be handily stored in a matrix as shown in Table 2.2. In this matrix we place the symbol p in the $(i, j)$ cell ($i$ = row number, $j$ = column number) when we have a relationship of $X_i > X_j$, otherwise we place the symbol x. The upper triangle cells in Table 2.2 denote the above 10 pairwise judgments. The lower triangle cells can be mechanically filled by the converse relationship. The last column, labeled $\sum C$, indicates the total number of p's in each row. In other words, $\sum C$ represents the frequency that an attribute is judged higher in the pairwise judgments. The attribute with the highest $\sum C$ is then ranked first and the attribute with the lowest $\sum C$ is

TABLE 2.2
Pairwise Judgments Between Attributes

|        | $X_1$ | $X_2$ | $X_3$ | $X_4$ | $X_5$ | $\sum C$ |
|--------|-------|-------|-------|-------|-------|----------|
| $X_1$  | –     | p     | p     | p     | p     | 4        |
| $X_2$  | x     | –     | x     | p     | x     | 1        |
| $X_3$  | x     | p     | –     | p     | x     | 2        |
| $X_4$  | x     | x     | x     | –     | x     | 0        |
| $X_5$  | x     | p     | p     | p     | –     | 3        |

then ranked last. Thus the complete ranking among five attributes is $[X_1,$ $X_5, X_3, X_2, X_4]$ where $X_1$ is ranked first and $X_4$ last.

If, in the above procedure, the preference statements had been $(X_1 > X_2)$, $(X_2 > X_4)$, and $(X_1 < X_4)$, the DM should reconsider the inconsistent judgments. These results are "intransitive" in a mathematical sense.

### 2.2.2. Ratio Weighting

These techniques compare two attributes at a time and ask for the preference (importance) ratio between them. For instance, "How many times is $X_i$ attribute more important than attribute $X_j$?" Mathematically we need $(n - 1)$ pairwise comparisons to establish the relative importance among $n$ attributes. It is quite likely that the pairwise comparisons will be inconsistent. Therefore, these approaches require more information to compensate for the inconsistencies of human judgment. Efficient techniques to retrieve weights from $n(n - 1)/2$ pairwise comparison data include the eigenvector prioritization method by Saaty (1980).

Saaty (1980) presented the simplified eigenvector prioritization method as follows:

*Step 1. Input Coding.* A DM assesses $n(n - 1)/2$ importance (weight) ratios between attributes. This information is stored in the upper (or lower) triangle of a $(n \times n)$ matrix whose typical element $a_{jk}$ represents the weight ratio of $w_j/w_k$. The remaining elements of the matrix are filled by employing the reciprocal property of the matrix: $a_{jk} = 1/a_{kj}$ and $a_{jj} = 1$, for all $j$ and $k$. For a numerical example assume that a DM made the following pairwise judgments among these attributes:

$$\begin{array}{c} \\ X_1 \\ X_2 \\ X_3 \end{array}\begin{array}{ccc} X_1 & X_2 & X_3 \end{array} \\ \begin{bmatrix} w_1/w_1 & w_1/w_2 & w_1/w_3 \\ w_2/w_1 & w_2/w_2 & w_2/w_3 \\ w_3/w_1 & w_3/w_2 & w_3/w_3 \end{bmatrix} = \begin{bmatrix} 1 & 1/3 & 1/2 \\ 3 & 1 & 3 \\ 2 & 1/3 & 1 \end{bmatrix}$$

*Step 2. Computing.* Compute the geometric mean of each row of the matrix, and then normalize the resulting numbers. That is,

$$\begin{array}{c} \\ X_1 \\ X_2 \\ X_3 \end{array}\begin{array}{cc} Geometric\,Mean & Weight \end{array} \\ \begin{bmatrix} (1 \times 1/3 \times 1/2)^{1/3} = 0.5503 \\ (3 \times 1 \times 3)^{1/3} = 2.0801 \\ (2 \times 1/3 \times 1)^{1/3} = 0.8736 \end{bmatrix} = \begin{bmatrix} 0.1571 \\ 0.5936 \\ 0.2493 \end{bmatrix} \\ \text{sum} = 3.5040 \qquad\quad 1.0000$$

## 2.3. Quantification of Qualitative Ratings

An alternative in a MADM problem is usually described by attributes that are either quantitative or qualitative. How do we compare these two kinds of attributes? If the number of qualitative attributes is much larger than the number of quantitative attributes, we convert quantitative into qualitative attributes and apply the Median Ranking method described in Chapter 7. Otherwise the assignment of numerical values to qualitative data (i.e., quantification) by scaling is the preferred approach.

The *Likert-type* scale (McIver & Carmines, 1981; Spector, 1992), which is probably the most suitable for our purposes, is described as follows. A set of statements, composed of approximately an equal number of favorable and unfavorable statements covering qualitative attributes, is constructed. For example, the attitude of residents toward the opening of a new plant can be aptly described on a five-point scale as *very unfavorable, unfavorable, neutral, favorable,* and *very favorable.* The DM is asked to pick a statement that best describes the given attribute property. To score the scale, the response statements are credited with 1, 2, 3, 4, or 5, reading from unfavorable to favorable. A five-point Likert-type scale has been applied predominantly in marketing and psychology literature (Anastasi, 1988; Lynch, 1985), but a more detailed scale such as a seven-point or nine-point scale might be more adequate depending on the decision problem context. Since the Likert-type scale is an interval scale, the intervals between statements are meaningful but ratios between scale scores have no meaning. Therefore, a scale system of (3, 5, 7, 9, 11) can be utilized instead of (1, 2, 3, 4, 5). Note that the difference between a very favorable and a favorable rating is the same as the difference between a favorable and a neutral rating, which in turn is the same as the difference between a neutral and an unfavorable rating. However, we cannot say that a favorable rating is twice as advantageous as an unfavorable rating since their ratio on a (1, 2, 3, 4, 5) scale is 2 (= 4/2), and the same ratio on a (3, 5, 7, 9, 11) scale is 1.8 (= 9/5).

The verbal terms used in describing the residents' attitude toward the opening of a new plant may not be appropriate to describe other qualitative attributes. For example if price is one of the attributes, the possible statements could be {very expensive, . . . , fair price, fairly cheap, . . . , extremely cheap}. Or, if size is one of the attributes, the possible statements could be {extremely small, very small, . . . , medium, medium large, . . . , extremely large}. For any type of attribute, we can always find a pair of words that represents extreme meanings, such as high versus low, good versus poor, small versus large, and so on. A set of 76 pairs of opposite words may be found in Osgood, Suci, and Tannenbaum (1975).

## 2.4. Normalization of Attribute Ratings

Attribute ratings are normalized to eliminate computational problems caused by differing measurement units in a decision matrix. It is not always necessary but is essential for many compensatory MADM methods. Normalization aims at obtaining comparable scales, which allow interattribute as well as intra-attribute comparisons. Consequently, normalized ratings have dimensionless units and, the larger the rating becomes, the more preference it has. We first classify attributes into three groups and then present normalization techniques for each group:

1. *Benefit attributes:* Offer increasing monotonic utility. That is, the greater the attribute value the more its preference; for example, fuel efficiency.
2. *Cost attributes:* Offer decreasing monotonic utility. That is, the greater the attribute value the less its preference; for example, production cost.
3. *Nonmonotonic attributes:* Offer nonmonotonic utility, such as the room temperature in an office, or the blood sugar level in a human body, where the maximum utility is located somewhere in the middle of an attribute range.

The normalization methods for benefit attributes are as follows:

1. *Linear Normalization.* A simple procedure that divides the ratings of a certain attribute by its maximum value. The normalized value of $x_{ij}$ is given as

$$r_{ij} = x_{ij}/x_j^*, \quad i = 1, \ldots, m; \quad j = 1, \ldots, n$$

where $x_j^*$ is the maximum value of the $j$th attribute. It is clear that $0 \le r_{ij} \le 1$, and the attribute is more favorable as $r_{ij}$ approaches 1.

2. *Vector Normalization.* This procedure divides the rating of each attribute by its norm, so that each normalized rating of $x_{ij}$ can be calculated as

$$r_{ij} = \frac{x_{ij}}{\sqrt{\sum_{i=1}^{m} x_{ij}^2}}, \quad i = 1, \ldots, m; \quad j = 1, \ldots, n.$$

The above normalization equations are for benefit attributes. Cost attributes can be transformed to benefit attributes by taking inverse ratings (i.e., $1/x_{ij}$). Then the transformed benefit attribute (from cost) follows the exact same normalization process. Note that cost normalization by the linear scale method takes the following simple form:

$$r_{ij} = \frac{1/x_{ij}}{\max_k\{1/x_{kj}\}} = \frac{1/x_{ij}}{1/\min_k\{x_{kj}\}} = \frac{\min_k\{x_{kj}\}}{x_{ij}} = \frac{x_j^-}{x_{ij}}$$

where $x_j^-$ is the minimum value of the $j$th attribute.

Nonmonotonic attributes become monotonic by taking the statistical $z$ score: $\exp(-z^2/2)$ where $z = (x_{ij} - x_j^0)/\sigma_j$, $x_j^0$ is the most favorable value, and $\sigma_j$ is the standard deviation of alternative ratings with respect to the $j$th attribute. Then the comparable rating is obtained by one of the normalization equations. A normalization for the number of rooms in a house is calculated in Table 2.3.

TABLE 2.3
Normalization for a Nonmonotonic Attribute

| Number of Rooms in a House | $z$ | $\exp(-z^2/2)$ | Normalization by Linear | Vector |
|---|---|---|---|---|
| 3 | −0.6324 | .8187 | .8187 | .5107 |
| 4* | 0.0000 | 1.0000 | 1.0000 | .6238 |
| 5 | .6324 | .8187 | .8187 | .5107 |
| 6 | 1.2649 | .4493 | .4493 | .2803 |
| 7 | 1.8974 | .1653 | .1653 | .0317 |

* indicates the optimum number of rooms determined by the DM.

## 3. NONCOMPENSATORY METHODS

A compensatory or noncompensatory distinction is made on the basis of whether advantages of one attribute can be traded for disadvantages of another or not. A choice strategy is compensatory if trade-offs among attribute values are permitted, otherwise it is noncompensatory. Therefore, compensatory strategies are cognitively more demanding but may lead to more optimal or at least more rational decision outcomes than do noncompensatory strategies.

In the noncompensatory model a superiority in one attribute cannot be offset by an inferiority in some other attribute(s). Each attribute must stand on its own. For instance, in scouting for football players, a player's kicking ability is irrelevant if he is chosen for his passing ability. Hence, comparisons are usually made on an attribute basis. Noncompensatory methods are credited for their simple logic and computation. However, the rationale behind each method is unique, and therefore it is essential to use an appropriate method in a given decision making context.

### 3.1. Dominance

Multiple attributes tend to conflict. In designing a car, for instance, reducing passenger space to achieve a goal of higher gas mileage might also decrease passenger comfort. Consequently, a wide variety of cars exist: compact cars with high gas mileage and poor comfort, full-size cars with low gas mileage and excellent comfort, and so on. These cars survive in the market because each one surpasses the others in at least one attribute. In other words they are nondominated with respect to each other.

TABLE 3.1
Decision Matrix for Seven Sites

| Sites | $X_1$ | $X_2$ | $X_3$ |
|-------|-------|-------|-------|
| $S_1$ | poor | good | 0.5 |
| $S_2$ | excellent | fair | 1.0 |
| $S_3$ | poor | poor | 1.0 |
| $S_4$ | fair | fair | 0.1 |
| $S_5$ | good | excellent | 0.2 |
| $S_6$ | fair | good | 0.9 |
| $S_7$ | good | fair | 1.0 |

NOTE: $X_1$ = community attitude, $X_2$ = water availability, $X_3$ = probability of a union within the next two years.
SOURCE: Yoon and Hwang (1985).

Formally, an alternative is *dominated* if there is another alternative that excels it in one or more attributes and equals it in the remaining attributes. Conversely, an alternative is *nondominated* (also called efficient frontier or Pareto Optimal) if there is no alternative that excels it in all the attributes considered. A set of nondominated alternatives is identified by making a number of pairwise comparisons: Compare the first two alternatives; if one is dominated by the other, discard the dominated one. Next, compare the undiscarded alternatives with the third alternative and discard any dominated alternative. Then introduce the fourth alternative, and so on. If we start with $m$ alternatives, a nondominated set is obtained after $(m-1)$ stages.

*Case 3.1. Site Selection for a Textile Company.* A textile manufacturing company wants to open a new plant in the state of North Carolina. Since the plant requires abundant water and manpower, the company believes that water availability, community attitude toward possible water pollution, and likelihood of union formation are the most pertinent location attributes affecting the plant. Seven sites judged by these attributes are presented in Table 3.1 (Yoon & Hwang, 1985).

The first site $S_1$ is compared with $S_2$. $S_1$ is better than $S_2$ in attributes $X_2$ and $X_3$ but worse than $S_2$ in $X_1$, therefore, they are not dominated by each other. Next, $S_3$ is compared with $S_1$. $S_3$ is worse than $S_1$ in $X_2$ and $X_3$ and equivalent to $S_1$ in $X_1$; $S_3$ is thus dominated by $S_1$ (expressed as $S_1 \rightarrow S_3$) and discarded. Then, $S_4$ is compared with $S_1$ and $S_2$, and found to be nondominated. The pairwise comparison for nondomination screening is continued until $S_7$ is reached. The complete dominance relationship through

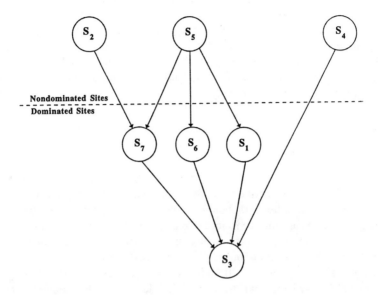

Figure 3.1. Domination Graph for Seven Sites
SOURCE: Chen and Hwang (1992).

pairwise comparisons is given in Figure 3.1. Since no arrow goes into $S_2$, $S_4$, and $S_5$, they are nondominated sites. The DM may pick one of the nondominated sites at random if his or her rationality is limited.

We as decision analysts have placed great emphasis on screening non-dominated alternatives, because any nondominated alternative can be regarded as a rational choice, if there is no information about the DM's preferences. However, McAnarney's (1987) study found that some dominated alternatives, which would get discarded, might overall be better than some of the nondominated alternatives. For instance, consider three alternatives that are evaluated by four benefit attributes:

$$
\begin{array}{c}
\quad\ \ X_1 \ X_2 \ X_3 \ X_4 \\
\begin{array}{c} A_1 \\ A_2 \\ A_3 \end{array}
\left[ \begin{array}{cccc}
7 & 8 & 5 & 8 \\
7 & 7 & 5 & 8 \\
4 & 3 & 6 & 5
\end{array} \right]
\end{array}
$$

Alternative $A_2$ is dominated by $A_1$ although it is nearly as good. Alternative $A_3$, on the other hand, is not dominated, but is much worse than $A_2$ on three out of four attributes. Overall, $A_2$ is much better than $A_3$ but would not get considered for selection because it is dominated. Therefore, to compensate for a possible error in judgment, we suggest the application of a Conjunctive method (Section 3.2.1) first, and nondominated screening next, to screen the alternatives effectively.

## 3.2. Satisficing Methods

There are two types of satisficing methods based on multiple attributes: Conjunctive and Disjunctive methods. These methods are not used to select an alternative but rather to dichotomize them into acceptable/unacceptable categories. Each alternative is acceptable as long as it meets the minimum cutoffs. For example, one can obtain a driver's license as long as he or she earns more than the minimum required scores/standards on various tests such as vision (e.g., at least 20/50 in New Jersey), rules of the road (e.g., at least 80% correct in a written test in New Jersey), health examinations, and driving tests. One does not need the highest scores to pass the tests. Therefore, the selections are *satisficing* (Simon, 1957) rather than optimizing.

### 3.2.1. Conjunctive Method

Consider, for example, the position of a visiting American history teacher in a French school (Dawes, 1964). An individual's effectiveness as a teacher will be limited by the lesser of his or her abilities in history and French; he or she cannot compensate for an insufficient knowledge of French by an excellent knowledge of history, or vice versa. The school wants to eliminate candidates who do not possess an acceptable knowledge of both subjects. Similarly, a car that meets all safety and emission standards can pass a motor vehicle inspection. To be chosen by this method, an alternative must exceed a minimum value on all attributes. Alternatives are easily rejected; they need fail only one attribute. Accordingly an alternative $A_i$ can be classified as an acceptable alternative only if

$$x_{ij} \geq x_j^0, \quad j = 1 \text{ and } 2 \ . \ . \ . \text{ and } n$$

where $x_j^0$ is the minimum acceptable level of the $j$th attribute.

TABLE 3.2
Graduate School Admission for International Students

| Students | TOEFL | GRE | GPA |
|----------|-------|-----|-----|
| $A_1$ | 582 | 1,420 | 2.8 |
| $A_2$ | 563 | 1,250 | 3.5 |
| $A_3$ | 620 | 1,080 | 3.2 |
| $A_4$ | 558 | 1,280 | 3.0 |
| . | . | . | . |
| . | . | . | . |
| . | . | . | . |
| $A_{50}$ | 600 | 1,210 | 3.6 |
| Minimum | 550 | 1,200 | 3.0 |

To apply this method, the DM must supply the minimal (cutoff) attribute values acceptable for each of the attributes. The cutoff values given by the DM play a key role in eliminating noncontender alternatives; if they are too high, none are left; if they are relatively low, quite a few alternatives are left. Hence, by increasing the minimal standard levels in an iterative way, we can sometimes narrow the alternatives down to a single choice.

*Case 3.2. Graduate School Admission for International Students.* A graduate school official screens international applicants for admission. To pass the screening, an applicant whose native language is not English must meet the minimum scores on three requirements: TOEFL (Test of English as a Foreign Language), GRE (Graduate Record Examination), and GPA (Grade Point Average). A simplified example is shown in Table 3.2. Students $A_1$ and $A_3$ are rejected due to their low GPA and GRE scores, respectively. Note that $A_1$ was rejected even though the candidate has a very high GRE score.

### 3.2.2. Disjunctive Method

Like the Conjunctive method, the Disjunctive method requires the DM to establish cutoff values for the attributes. An alternative is chosen if and only if it exceeds a minimal cutoff on one or more attributes. Individuals can be viewed from a disjunctive viewpoint. As long as an individual is good in any field he or she can qualify for selection. For instance, one might be employed for his or her good engineering skills, while another might survive because he or she is good at painting. We classify $A_i$ as an acceptable alternative only if

$$x_{ij} \geq x_j^0, \quad j = 1 \; or \; 2 \; \ldots \; or \; n$$

where $x_j^0$ is a desirable level of the $j$th attribute.

In the disjunctive form, where only one standard needs to be exceeded, most alternatives will pass unless the standards are set at or near the maximal level. If all alternatives are disqualified, the DM can reduce the cutoffs of one or more attributes and resume the evaluation of alternatives.

The Disjunctive method is usually utilized in conjunction with the Conjunctive method. A good example is found from an advertisement for a faculty position:

> Tenure-line position in Applied Ethics, with rank open. Successful candidate will assume a major role in Stanford's Ethics in Society Program. Requirements include expertise and scholarship in ethics or political philosophy, and the proven aptitude to apply such thinking to one or more areas, such as law, medicine, public policy, international relations, business or technological, global or environmental issues.

An acceptable applicant should possess one expertise and one application area (conjunctive constraint) but has two options within the expertise and many options within the application area (disjunctive constraint).

## 3.3. Sequential Elimination Methods

There are two MADM methods that eliminate alternatives in a sequential manner. Both methods use one attribute at a time to examine alternatives for elimination. After all the alternatives are examined, if more than one still remains, the process is repeated using another attribute. The Lexicographic method examines alternatives in the order of attribute importance, whereas Elimination by Aspects does so in the order of attributes that would eliminate the most alternatives.

### 3.3.1. Lexicographic Methods

In some decision situations a single attribute seems to predominate. For example, "Buy the cheapest" is a rule where price is the most important attribute to the DM. "Quality is job 1," a commercial slogan for the Ford Motor Company, is another example, in which the attribute "quality" prevails over other attributes. One way of treating this situation is to compare alternatives on the most important attribute. If one alternative has a higher (or more preferable) attribute value than any of the other alternatives, that alternative is chosen and the decision process ends. However, if some alternatives are tied on the most important attribute, the subset of tied alternatives are then compared on the next most important attribute. The process continues sequentially until a single alternative is chosen or until all attributes have been considered. The term "lexicography" reflects the similarity between this method and the manner in which words are ordered in a dictionary.

Let $X_1$ be the most important attribute to the DM, $X_2$ the second most important one, and so on. Then alternative $A^1$ is selected such that

$$A^1 = \left\{ A_i \mid \max_i x_{i1} \right\}, \quad i = 1, 2, \ldots, m.$$

If the set $\{A^1\}$ has a single element, then this element is the most preferred alternative. If there remain multiple alternatives, consider

$$A^2 = \left\{ A^1 \mid \max_i x_{i2} \right\}, \quad i \in \left\{ A^1 \right\}.$$

If the set $\{A^2\}$ has a single element, then stop and select this alternative. Otherwise continue this process until either some $\{A^k\}$ with a single element is found or all attributes have been considered. If the remaining set contains more than one alternative, they are considered to be equivalent.

*Case 3.3. World Rankings in the 1992 Summer Olympic Games.* Table 3.3 shows the number of gold, silver, and bronze medals each nation earned in the 1992 Summer Olympics. The lexicographic principle was used to rank nations based on the total number of medals they received. In the event of a tie, a comparison of the number of gold medals received determined the ranking. If another tie resulted, the number of silver medals received were considered. For example, South Korea and France received an equal number of total medals (29), however South Korea had a greater number of gold medals (12) than France (8), which gave South Korea a higher overall ranking.

TABLE 3.3
Medals Table in 1992 Summer Olympic Games

| Rank | Country | G | S | B | Total |
|------|---------|---|---|---|-------|
| 1 | Unified Team | 45 | 38 | 29 | 112 |
| 2 | United States | 37 | 34 | 37 | 108 |
| 3 | Germany | 33 | 21 | 28 | 82 |
| 4 | China | 16 | 22 | 16 | 54 |
| 5 | Cuba | 14 | 6 | 11 | 31 |
| 6 | Hungary | 11 | 12 | 7 | 30 |
| 7 | South Korea | 12 | 5 | 12 | 29 |
| 8 | France | 8 | 5 | 16 | 29 |
| 9 | Australia | 7 | 9 | 11 | 27 |
| 10 | Spain | 13 | 7 | 2 | 22 |

NOTE: G = gold, S = silver, B = bronze.

*Case 3.4. Family Automobile Selection.* A family wants to purchase a car and has narrowed its search down to eight candidates. Their ratings are based on six attributes as given in Table 3.4. After due consideration, the family decides the priority of attribute importance to be: Attribute $X_6$ (handling), followed by $X_1$ (list price), followed by $X_5$ (acceleration), and so on. Five alternatives $\{A_1, A_2, A_3, A_4, A_7\}$ are tied for the first position based on attribute $X_6$. The lexicographic method reduces this set by considering the next important attribute, $X_1$. Alternative $A_1$ is selected because it has the lowest list price ($1,359 less than the next cheapest alternative, $A_2$).

The *Lexicographic Semiorder* (LS) method, described by Luce (1956) and Tversky (1969), uses the same logic as the Lexicographic method except that an alternative is judged to be distinct only when it is significantly different from the rest. For example, an employer who regards intelligence as being more important than experience may view one candidate as being brighter than another only if the difference between their IQ scores exceeds 10 points. If the difference between the applicants IQ scores is less than 10 points, the employer considers the applicants to be equally bright and selects the more experienced candidate. Such a decision rule is particularly appealing when the relevant attribute is noisy because of imperfect discrimination or the unreliability of available information. Thus, in addition to the order of importance of the attributes, a consideration of bands of imperfect discrimination (e.g., 10 points in IQ) is imposed on the LS method.

TABLE 3.4

Decision Matrix for Automobile Evaluation

| Cars | $X_1$ | $X_2$ | $X_3$ | $X_4$ | $X_5$ | $X_6$ |
|------|-------|-------|-------|-------|-------|-------|
| $A_1$ | 8,307 | 3,000 | 5.0 | 18.0 | 14.7 | 7.0 |
| $A_2$ | 9,666 | 3,600 | 5.0 | 12.0 | 19.1 | 7.0 |
| $A_3$ | 10,578 | 3,600 | 7.0 | 10.0 | 10.8 | 7.0 |
| $A_4$ | 13,695 | 6,000 | 2.5 | 9.0 | 13.0 | 7.0 |
| $A_5$ | 29,844 | 12,000 | 6.0 | 11.0 | 13.7 | 4.0 |
| $A_6$ | 11,037 | 3,600 | 7.0 | 19.0 | 16.2 | 4.0 |
| $A_7$ | 9,807 | 3,600 | 5.0 | 12.0 | 15.3 | 7.0 |
| $A_8$ | 27,642 | 12,000 | 6.0 | 10.0 | 13.5 | 1.0 |

NOTE: $X_1$ = list price ($), $X_2$ = resale value ($), $X_3$ = maintainability (*), $X_4$ = city mileage (mpg), $X_5$ = acceleration (sec), $X_6$ = handling (*); * units are on a 10-point scale, from 1 (worst) to 10 (best).

The family automobile selection of Case 3.4 is revisited with the LS method. After reviewing the lexicographic evaluation process, a member of the family decides that a price differential of $1,359 between $A_1$ and $A_2$ is insignificant and suggests further evaluation of alternatives that are slightly higher priced. The family accepts the suggestion and adopts the LS method. Their threshold values of significance for each attribute are: more than 2 points for $X_6$, more than $3,000 for $X_1$, more than 3 seconds for $X_5$, and so on. The alternatives $\{A_1, A_2, A_3, A_4, A_7\}$ are tied based on $X_6$, and no other alternative lies within a 2 point difference. $A_1$ has the lowest list price ($X_1$) of $8,307. Now, given the threshold value of significance for price ($3,000), the family can further evaluate alternatives that cost up to $11,307. Four alternatives $\{A_1, A_2, A_3, A_7\}$ remain after $A_4$, priced at $13,695, is dropped. For acceleration ($X_5$), $A_3$ has the best rating (10.8 sec.) and none of the remaining alternatives $\{A_1, A_2, A_7\}$ falls within the threshold value of significance for acceleration (3 seconds) to be considered any further. Since only one car, $A_3$, is left, it is chosen to be the family car.

### 3.3.2. Elimination by Aspects

A procedure very similar to the Lexicographic method is the Elimination by Aspects (EBA) suggested by Tversky (1972). Like Lexicography, it examines one attribute at a time, making comparisons among alternatives. However, it differs slightly because it eliminates alternatives that do not satisfy some standard, and it continues until all alternatives except one have been eliminated. Another difference is that the attributes are not ordered in terms of importance but in terms of their probabilistic discrimination power. That is, attributes are examined in the order of likelihood for more alternatives to fail. As an illustration of EBA, Tversky describes a television commercial that advertises a computer course:

> "There are more than two dozen companies in the San Francisco area which offer training in computer programming."
> The announcer puts two dozen eggs and one walnut on the table to represent the alternatives, and continues:
> "Let us examine the facts. How many of these schools have on-line computer facilities for training?"
> The announcer removes several eggs.
> "How many of these schools have placement services that would help find you a job?"
> The announcer removes some more eggs.
> "How many of these schools are approved for veterans' benefits?"
> This continues until the walnut alone remains. The announcer cracks open the walnut, which reveals the name of the company, and concludes:
> "This is all you need to know in a nutshell."

In the above example, alternatives are eliminated by the aspects of "on-line computer facilities for training," "placement services," and "approval for veterans' benefits." These aspects could represent quantitative or qualitative attributes (e.g., price, comfort), or they could be features of the alternatives that do not fit into any simple dimensional structure (e.g., a luxury edition car that has power steering, cruise control, etc.).

Let $X_1$ be the most effective aspect to eliminate the greatest number of alternatives, $X_2$ the second most effective one, and so on. Then alternative $A^1$ is screened such that

$$A^1 = \{A_i \mid x_{i1} \text{ satisfies } X_1\}, \quad i = 1, 2, \ldots, m.$$

If the set $\{A^1\}$ has a single element, then this element is the most preferred alternative. If there are multiple elements, consider the next important aspect $X_2$:

$$A^2 = \{A^1 \mid x_{i2} \text{ satisfies } X_2\}, \quad i \in \{A^1\}.$$

If the set $\{A^2\}$ has a single element, then stop and select this alternative, otherwise consider the next important aspect $X_3$, and so on.

TABLE 3.5
Long Distance Phone Company Selection

| Companies | $X_1$ | $X_2$ | $X_3$ | $X_4$ | $X_5$ |
|-----------|-------|-------|-------|-------|-------|
| $A_1$ | Y | Y | N | Y | Y |
| $A_2$ | N | Y | N | Y | Y |
| $A_3$ | Y | Y | Y | Y | Y |
| $A_4$ | Y | N | N | Y | Y |

NOTE: $X_1$ = operator service, $X_2$ = immediate credit for a wrong number, $X_3$ = worldwide call, $X_4$ = clear connection, $X_5$ = daytime discount up to 70%; Y = yes, N = no (not available).
SOURCE: Nagashima (1986).

*Case 3.5. Long Distance Phone Company Selection.* A customer wants to select a long distance phone company (Nagashima, 1986). Four companies are contrasted over five aspects (or attributes) as shown in Table 3.5. The customers' order of preference on aspects is: daytime discount ($X_5$), immediate credit ($X_2$), operator service ($X_1$), worldwide calling ($X_3$), and clear connection ($X_4$). The selection process is depicted below:

| Order of aspect | Remaining alternatives | | | |
|:---:|:---:|:---:|:---:|:---:|
| $X_5$ | $A_1$ | $A_2$ | $A_3$ | $A_4$ |
| $X_2$ | $A_1$ | $A_2$ | $A_3$ | ~~$A_4$~~ |
| $X_1$ | $A_1$ | ~~$A_2$~~ | $A_3$ | |
| $X_3$ | ~~$A_1$~~ | | $A_3$ | |

where alternatives that do not possess the required aspect are crossed out. Company $A_3$ remains as the alternative that satisfies all the aspects.

## 3.4. Attitude Oriented Methods

There are two noncompensatory MADM methods that consider the DM's attitude toward the decision environment. When the DM has a pessimistic attitude, the Maximin method is used to identify the worst attribute of each alternative and pick an alternative that has the best of the worst attribute ratings. When the DM has an optimistic attitude, the Maximax method is used to select an alternative with the best of the best ratings.

### 3.4.1. Maximin

A chain is only as strong as its weakest link. Similarly, an astronaut's life or death in orbit may depend upon his or her worst vital organ. The overall performance of an alternative is determined by its weakest or poorest attribute. In such a situation, where a DM does not have prior knowledge as to which attribute will determine overall performance (or which link will yield first), the DM should take a pessimistic attitude and choose that alternative whose worst rating is better than the worst rating of the others. It is the selection of the maximum (across alternatives) of the minimum (across attributes) values, which is called "maximin" or "best of the worst."

Under this procedure only a single weakest (or worst) attribute represents an alternative; all other attributes of the alternative are ignored. If these lowest attribute values come from different attributes, as they often do, we may be basing our final choice on single ratings of attributes that differ from alternative to alternative. In the selection of an astronaut, for instance, suppose that one candidate's weakest organ is the heart and another candidate's weakest organ is the lung. We cannot compare a heart with a lung unless we have a common scale to measure their survivabilities. Therefore, the Maximin method can be used only when interattribute values are comparable; this necessitates converting all attribute values to a common (not necessarily numerical) scale.

The selection procedure has two steps: Determine the poorest attribute value for each alternative, then select that alternative with the best value on the poorest attribute. In mathematical notation an alternative $A^+$ is selected such that

$$A^+ = \left\{A_i \mid \max_i \min_j r_{ij}\right\}$$

where $r_{ij}$ is a comparable scale of $x_{ij}$.

*Case 3.6. Selection of a Manager.* A growing electronics manufacturing company needs to select a manager for its newly established South American division. The manager will be stationed in Brazil and will be responsible for the operation of the new division. The vice president of personnel reviews six candidates for the position and evaluates them on the basis of five attributes. The evaluation data are presented in Table 3.6. Attribute ratings are based on a 10-point scale with a larger-greater preference.

TABLE 3.6
Decision Matrix for Six Managers

| Candidates | $X_1$ | $X_2$ | $X_3$ | $X_4$ | $X_5$ |
|------------|-------|-------|-------|-------|-------|
| $A_1$ | 4 | 6 | 3 | 2 | 3 |
| $A_2$ | 7 | 2 | 8 | 2 | 4 |
| $A_3$ | 8 | 5 | 4 | 6 | 3 |
| $A_4$ | 6 | 7 | 5 | 5 | 6 |
| $A_5$ | 3 | 5 | 6 | 8 | 7 |
| $A_6$ | 8 | 9 | 2 | 8 | 8 |

NOTE: $X_1$ = leadership, $X_2$ = organization planning, $X_3$ = foreign language, $X_4$ = job knowledge, $X_5$ = decision making.

The president of the company (male) agrees with the evaluation criteria; however, he cannot judge which attribute would most affect the manager's performance. Hence, he suggests the selection of a "catch all" candidate for the position. The personnel department therefore uses the Maximin method to select a manager who has the strongest of the weakest attributes. Since all ratings are on a 10-point scale, comparisons can be made directly across attributes. First we find the minimum rating for each candidate (rows), and then choose the maximum among the minimums. The procedure is shown below:

$$
\begin{array}{c}
 & X_1 & X_2 & X_3 & X_4 & X_5 & \text{min} \\
A_1 & 4 & 6 & 3 & 2 & 3 & 2 \\
A_2 & 7 & 2 & 8 & 2 & 4 & 2 \\
A_3 & 8 & 5 & 4 & 6 & 3 & 3 \\
A_4 & 6 & 7 & 5 & 5 & 6 & 5 \leftarrow \text{max} \\
A_5 & 3 & 5 & 6 & 8 & 7 & 3 \\
A_6 & 8 & 9 & 2 & 8 & 8 & 2
\end{array}
$$

Candidate $A_4$ (male) is chosen for the position. Note that his performance does not go below 5 points in any attribute, whereas other candidates have one or more weak attributes.

This method utilized only a small part of the available information in making a final choice—only one attribute per alternative. Thus, even if an alternative is clearly superior in all but one attribute, which is below average, another alternative with only an average on all attributes would be chosen over it. Compare the chosen candidate $A_4$ with candidate $A_6$, who has excellent ratings in all attributes except $X_3$ in our example. In a general decision making situation a Maximin method would be reasonable only if the DM assumed that some malevolent nature was trying to inflict the worst possible outcome on him or her. Any DM who believes this and makes his or her choice accordingly deserves the outcome he or she will receive (MacCrimmon, 1968).

### 3.4.2. Maximax

In contrast to the Maximin method, the Maximax method selects an alternative by its best attribute rating rather than its worst. This method is particularly useful when the alternatives can be specialized in use based upon one attribute and the DM has no prior requirement as to which attribute this is. Consider for example a talent contest for discovering an entertainment star. One contestant may be excellent in singing, another in dancing, yet another in comedy, and so on. The panel of judges would identify each contestant's one outstanding talent and then pick the contestant with the most outstanding talent. It follows that a candidate with an average talent in several areas cannot be a star. Similarly, professional football players are selected according to the Maximax method; a player is selected because he can either pass exceptionally, run exceptionally, or kick exceptionally. A player's passing ability is irrelevant if he is chosen for his kicking ability (Dawes, 1964).

In the Maximax method only a single attribute represents an alternative, and all other attributes are ignored. Therefore, this method, too, requires comparability among attributes. The Maximax has two operating procedures: Identify the best attribute value for each alternative, then select the alternative with the maximum of the best values. In mathematical notation, an alternative, $A^+$ is selected such that

$$A^+ = \left\{ A_i \mid \max_i \max_j r_{ij} \right\}$$

The electronic manufacturing company, which we considered in Case 3.6, has another manager selection problem. The first manager returns after 2 years of directing operations in Brazil. He reports an economic climate of growth coupled with severe competition. This time the president wants to select a candidate who possesses top-notch management skills and a deputy to compensate for his or her weakest attribute. The president's selection policy can be interpreted as choosing the "best of the best"; which can be carried out using the Maximax method. First we determine the best rating of each candidate, then we select a candidate who has the best of the best ratings. The evaluation process of seven candidates is given below:

$$
\begin{array}{c}
 \\
A_7 \\
A_8 \\
A_9 \\
A_{10} \\
A_{11} \\
A_{12} \\
A_{13}
\end{array}
\begin{array}{ccccc}
X_1 & X_2 & X_3 & X_4 & X_5 \\
\left[\begin{array}{ccccc}
3 & 4 & 6 & 3 & 2 \\
8 & 8 & 2 & 8 & 9 \\
7 & 4 & 6 & 5 & 5 \\
7 & 2 & 2 & 8 & 4 \\
4 & 6 & 8 & 2 & 7 \\
5 & 7 & 4 & 5 & 6 \\
8 & 7 & 2 & 8 & 5
\end{array}\right]
\end{array}
\begin{array}{l}
\text{max} \\
6 \\
9 \leftarrow \text{max} \\
7 \\
8 \\
8 \\
7 \\
8
\end{array}
$$

Candidate $A_8$ (female) is selected because of her high decision making ability ($X_5$). Later, to compensate for her weakest attribute ($X_3$), the president can select a deputy who is fluent in the foreign language.

## 4. SCORING METHODS

An alternative in a MADM problem may be viewed as a vector having multiple elements. The transformation of a vector to an appropriate scalar value is a MADM solution approach. We then select the alternative that has the highest value, or utility.

When we thoroughly understand the functional relationships within a system, we may formulate an index to represent its effectiveness. Meteorologists, for instance, realized that temperature alone did not represent the coldness of a winter. Therefore, they created the windchill factor index from a combination of temperature and wind speed to measure the cooling effect of the wind. In an example of R&D evaluation, the economic value of a project was formulated as $V = x_1 x_2 x_3 x_4 x_5 x_6 / x_7$ where $x_1$ = annual sales volume derived from the project, $x_2$ = profit per unit, $x_3$ = life span of the product in years, $x_7$ = total project cost, and $x_4$, $x_5$, $x_6$ are the probabilities of research, development, and market success, respectively (Souder, 1978).

When we have data from previous decisions we can use regression analysis to predict future performance. For instance, Dawes (1971) obtained the following performance index for the graduate school admission decision: $S = 0.006 \, \text{GRE} + 0.76 \, \text{GPA} + 0.2518 \, \text{QI}$, where QI is the quality of the undergraduate institution. The administration staff then select students who have high scores based on the index.

Up to now, we have discussed the possibility of an index formulation of a system when the DM has a thorough understanding of the functional relationships among its components, or when he or she possesses sufficient data to regress a statistical relationship. Since we cannot expect that any of these conditions will be met easily in a normal decision making environment, this chapter presents two scoring techniques: The Simple Additive Weighting method, which obtains an index by adding contributions from each attribute, and the Weighted Product method, which obtains the index by multiplying contributions from attributes.

## 4.1. Simple Additive Weighting (SAW) Method

The SAW method is probably the best known and most widely used MADM method. A score in the SAW method is obtained by adding contributions from each attribute. Since two items with different measurement units cannot be added, a common numerical scaling system such as normalization is required to permit addition among attribute values. The total score for each alternative then can be computed by multiplying the comparable rating for each attribute by the importance weight assigned to the attribute and then summing these products over all the attributes.

An early application of the SAW method can be found in the Constitution of the United States. Article I, Section 2 states that:

> Representatives and direct Taxes shall be apportioned among the several States which may be included within this Union, according to their respective Numbers, which shall be determined by adding to the whole Number of free Persons, including those bound to Service for a Term of Years, and excluding Indians not taxed, three fifths of all other Persons.

The founding fathers assigned weights of 1 to free persons, 0 to Indians, and $\frac{3}{5}$ to all others, which were then added to determine the degree of a State's representation in the Union.

Formally the value of an alternative in the SAW method can be expressed as

$$V(A_i) = V_i = \sum_{j=1}^{n} w_j \, v_j \, (x_{ij}), \qquad i = 1, \ldots, m$$

where $V(A_i)$ is the value function of alternative $A_i$, and $w_j$ and $v_j(\cdot)$ are weight and value functions of attribute $X_j$, respectively. Through the normalization process, each incommensurable attribute becomes a pseudo-value function, which allows direct addition among attributes. The value of alternative $A_i$ can be rewritten as

$$V_i = \sum_{j=1}^{n} w_j r_{ij}, \quad i = 1, \ldots, m$$

where $r_{ij}$ is the comparable scale of $x_{ij}$, which can be obtained by a normalization process.

The underlying assumption of the SAW method is that attributes are preferentially independent. Less formally, this means that the contribution of an individual attribute to the total (multiattribute) score is independent of other attribute values. Therefore, the DM's preference (or feelings) regarding the value of one attribute are not influenced in any way by the values of the other attributes (Fishburn, 1976). Fortunately, studies (Edwards, 1977; Farmer, 1987) show that the SAW method yields extremely close approximations to "true" value functions even when independence among attributes does not exactly hold.

In addition to the preference independence assumption, the SAW has a required characteristic for weights. That is, the SAW presumes that weights are proportional to the relative value of a unit change in each attribute's value function (Hobbs, 1980). For instance, let us consider a value function with two attributes: $V = w_1 v_1 + w_2 v_2$. By setting the amount of $V$ constant, we can derive the relationship of $w_1/w_2 = -\Delta v_2/\Delta v_1$. This relationship indicates that if $w_1 = 0.33$ and $w_2 = 0.66$, the DM must be indifferent to the trade between 2 units of $v_1$ and 1 unit of $v_2$. In our analogy of the Constitution, each State should be willing to trade three free persons for five other persons.

*Case 4.1. Military Fighter Selection Decision.* A country in the Pacific Rim decides to reinforce its air force by purchasing sophisticated jet fighters from the United States. Five competing models are available for purchase. The huge acquisition cost and long-term impact on national security force the acquisition officers to make circumspect decisions. They proceed to generate selection criteria by way of a goal hierarchy. The hierarchy for a good fighter is shown in Figure 4.1. Four mutually exclusive

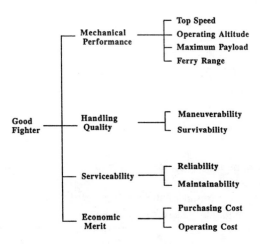

Figure 4.1. A Hierarchy for Fighter Evaluation

objectives are generated: mechanical performance, handling quality, ser-
viceability, and economic merit. Ten attributes emerge from these four
criteria. Evaluation data for five alternative models based on these ten
attributes are shown in Table 4.1.

First, a comparable rating is obtained by using any of the normalization
equations presented in Section 2.4. Linear normalization is most often used
with the SAW method. Note that only attributes $X_{41}$ and $X_{42}$ are cost
attributes. The normalized decision matrix is given as

$$
\begin{array}{cccccc}
 & X_{11} & X_{12} & X_{13} & \ldots & X_{41} & X_{42} \\
A_1 & \begin{bmatrix} 0.80 & 1.00 & 1.00 & \cdots & 1.00 & 0.78 \\ 0.80 & 0.83 & 0.87 & \cdots & 0.90 & 0.78 \\ 1.00 & 1.00 & 0.78 & \cdots & 0.69 & 0.70 \\ 0.80 & 0.83 & 0.87 & \cdots & 0.82 & 0.88 \\ 0.72 & 0.83 & 0.91 & \cdots & 0.90 & 1.00 \end{bmatrix}
\end{array}
$$

where columns of $X_{14}, X_{21}, X_{22}, X_{31},$ and $X_{32}$ are not shown here. The SAW
method needs a proper set of attribute weights. Instead of considering all
attributes at one time, the DM first considers four major criteria, then

TABLE 4. 1

Data for Evaluation of Fighters

| Attribute | Weight | $A_1$ | $A_2$ | $A_3$ | $A_4$ | $A_5$ |
|---|---|---|---|---|---|---|
| | | | | *Alternatives* | | |
| 1. Mechanical performance | | | | | | |
| 1.1 Top speed (Mach) | 0.20 | 2.0 | 2.0 | 2.5 | 2.0 | 1.8 |
| 1.2 Operating altitude (1,000 ft) | 0.04 | 60 | 50 | 60 | 50 | 50 |
| 1.3 Maximum payload (1,000 pounds) | 0.04 | 23 | 20 | 18 | 20 | 21 |
| 1.4 Ferry range (NM) | 0.12 | 1,900 | 2,000 | 3,500 | 2,400 | 2,300 |
| 2. Handling quality | | | | | | |
| 2.1 Maneuverability(*) | 0.09 | 7 | 8 | 8 | 9 | 9 |
| 2.2 Survivability(*) | 0.21 | 8 | 9 | 7 | 8 | 8 |
| 3. Serviceability | | | | | | |
| 3.1 Reliability(*) | 0.12 | 8 | 7 | 9 | 8 | 8 |
| 3.2 Maintainability(*) | 0.08 | 9 | 7 | 8 | 7 | 7 |
| 4. Economic merit | | | | | | |
| 4.1 Purchasing cost ($M/ea) | 0.06 | 4.5 | 5.0 | 6.5 | 5.5 | 5.0 |
| 4.2 Operating cost ($1,000/year) | 0.04 | 90 | 90 | 100 | 80 | 70 |

NOTE: Weights are obtained from Figure 4.2.
* units are from a 10-point scale, from 1 (worst) to 10 (best).

judges each attribute within each criterion. A tree structure is used to obtain the final weights. The final weights for attributes at each twig of the tree are obtained by multiplying through the branches. Figure 4.2 shows the entire weight assessment process.

The value of alternative $A_1$ is then computed as:

$$V(A_1) = \sum_{j=1}^{10} w_j \, r_{ij}$$

$$= 0.2(.8) + 0.04(1.0) + \ldots + 0.04(.78) = 0.8396.$$

The other alternatives have values of $V(A_2) = 0.8274$, $V(A_3) = 0.8953$, $V(A_4) = 0.8400$, and $V(A_5) = 0.8323$. The preference order is $[A_3, A_4, A_1, A_5, A_2]$, where $A_3$ is the first rank and $A_2$ is the last.

36

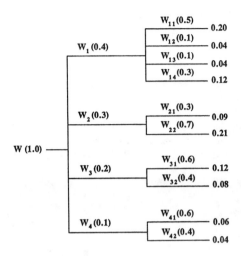

Figure 4.2. Weight Assessment for Fighter Evaluation

## 4.2. Weighted Product Method

In the SAW method, addition among attribute values was allowed only after the different measurement units were transformed into a dimensionless scale by a normalization process. However, this transformation is not necessary if attributes are connected by multiplication. When we use multiplication among attribute values, the weights become exponents associated with each attribute value; a positive power for benefit attributes, and a negative power for cost attributes. Formally, the value of alternative $A_i$ is given by

$$V(A_i) = V_i = \prod_{j=1}^{n} x_{ij}^{w_j}, \quad i = 1, \ldots, m.$$

Because of the exponent property, this method requires that all ratings be greater than 1. For instance, when an attribute has fractional ratings, all ratings in that attribute are multiplied by $10^m$ to meet this requirement. For example, the probabilities of union formation ($X_3$) in Table 3.1 should be changed to (5, 10, 10, 1, 2, 9, 10) before applying this method.

Alternative values obtained by the multiplicative method do not have a numerical upper bound. The DM may also not find any true meaning in those values. Hence, it may be convenient to compare each alternative value with the standard value. If we use the ideal alternative $A^*$ (see Section 5.1) for the comparison purpose, the value ratio between an alternative and the ideal alternative is given by

$$R_i = \frac{V(A_i)}{V(A^*)} = \frac{\prod\limits_{j=1}^{n} x_{ij}^{w_j}}{\prod\limits_{j=1}^{n} (x_j^*)^{w_j}}, \qquad i = 1, \ldots, m$$

where $x_j^*$ is the most favorable value for the $j$th attribute. It is clear that $0 \leq R_i \leq 1$ and the preference of $A_i$ increases when $R_i$ approaches 1.

Consider Case 4.1, the military fighter selection problem again. The value of alternative $A_1$ is obtained as

$$V(A_1) = (2.0)^{.2} (60)^{.04} \ldots (90)^{-.04} = 8.1716.$$

The other alternatives have values of $V(A_2) = 8.0707$, $V(A_3) = 8.7689$, $V(A_4) = 8.2565$, and $V(A_5) = 8.1485$. The preference order is $[A_3, A_4, A_1, A_5, A_2]$, which is identical with the order obtained by the SAW method for this case. The ratios with the ideal alternative are obtained as

$$(R_1, R_2, R_3, R_4, R_5) = (0.8274, 0.8172, 0.8575, 0.8363, 0.8251).$$

The weighted product method was introduced long ago by Bridgman (1922) and recently has been advocated by Starr (1972) and Yoon (1989). The method possesses sound logic and a simple computational process, but it has not yet been widely utilized.

# 5. TOPSIS

A MADM problem with $m$ alternatives that are evaluated by $n$ attributes may be viewed as a geometric system with $m$ points in the $n$-dimensional space. Hwang and Yoon (1981) developed the Technique for Order Preference by Similarity to Ideal Solution (TOPSIS) based on the concept that the chosen alternative should have the shortest distance from the positive-ideal solution and the longest distance from the negative-ideal solution. Lately, this principle has been also suggested by Zeleny (1982) and Hall (1989), and it has been enriched by Yoon (1987) and Hwang, Lai, and Liu (1993).

## 5.1. Positive-Ideal and Negative-Ideal Solutions

An ideal solution is defined as a collection of ideal levels (or ratings) in all attributes considered. However, the ideal solution is usually unattainable or infeasible. Then to be as close as possible to such an ideal solution is the *rationale of human choice*. Coombs (1958, 1964) also claimed that there is an ideal level of attributes for alternatives of choice and that the DM's utilities decrease monotonically when an alternative moves away from this ideal (or utopia) point (Yu, 1985). Since the ideal is dependent on the current limits and constraints of economy and technology, a perceived ideal is utilized instead to implement the choice rationale in a normative decision process. Formally the positive-ideal solution is denoted as

$$A^* = (x_1^*, \ldots, x_j^*, \ldots, x_n^*)$$

where $x_j^*$ is the best value for the $j$th attribute among all available alternatives.

The composite of all best attribute ratings attainable is the positive-ideal solution, whereas the negative-ideal solution is composed of all worst attribute ratings attainable. The negative-ideal solution is given as

$$A^- = (x_1^-, \ldots, x_j^-, \ldots, x_n^-)$$

where $x_j^-$ is the worst value for the $j$th attribute among all alternatives. Then does the chosen alternative that is closest to the positive-ideal solution concur with the chosen alternative that is farthest from the negative-ideal

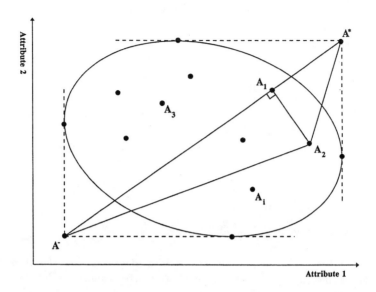

Figure 5.1. Euclidean Distances to Positive-Ideal and Negative-Ideal Solutions in Two-Dimensional Space
SOURCE: Hwang and Yoon (1981).

solution? Often they do not concur with each other. For example, consider two alternatives $A_1$ and $A_2$ with respect to two benefit attributes in Figure 5.1. $A_1$ is the closest to $A^*$ but $A_2$ is the farthest from $A^-$.

## 5.2. TOPSIS

TOPSIS defines an index called similarity (or relative closeness) to the positive-ideal solution by combining the proximity to the positive-ideal solution and the remoteness from the negative-ideal solution. Then the method chooses an alternative with the maximum similarity to the positive-ideal solution. TOPSIS assumes that each attribute takes either monotonically increasing or monotonically decreasing utility. That is, the larger the attribute outcome, the greater the preference for benefit attributes and the less the preference for cost attributes.

The method is presented as a series of successive steps:

*Step 1. Calculate Normalized Ratings.* The vector normalization is used for computing $r_{ij}$, which is given as

$$r_{ij} = \frac{x_{ij}}{\sqrt{\sum\limits_{i=1}^{m} x_{ij}^2}} \quad , \quad i = 1, \ldots, m; \quad j = 1, \ldots, n.$$

*Step 2. Calculate Weighted Normalized Ratings.* The weighted normalized value is calculated as

$$v_{ij} = w_j r_{ij}, \quad i = 1, \ldots, m; \quad j = 1, \ldots, n$$

where $w_j$ is the weight of the $j$th attribute.

*Step 3. Identify Positive-Ideal and Negative-Ideal Solutions.* The $A^*$ and $A^-$ are defined in terms of the weighted normalized values:

$$A^* = \left\{ v_1^*, v_2^*, \ldots, v_j^*, \ldots, v_n^* \right\}$$

$$= \left\{ (\max_i v_{ij} \mid j \in J_1), (\min_i v_{ij} \mid j \in J_2) \mid i = 1, \ldots, m \right\}$$

$$A^- = \left\{ v_1^-, v_2^-, \ldots, v_j^-, \ldots, v_n^- \right\}$$

$$= \left\{ (\min_i v_{ij} \mid j \in J_1), (\max_i v_{ij} \mid j \in J_2) \mid i = 1, \ldots, m \right\}$$

where $J_1$ is a set of benefit attributes and $J_2$ is a set of cost attributes.

*Step 4. Calculate Separation Measures.* The separation (distance) between alternatives can be measured by the $n$-dimensional Euclidean distance. The separation of each alternative from the positive-ideal solution, $A^*$, is then given by

$$S_i^* = \sqrt{\sum_{j=1}^{n} (v_{ij} - v_j^*)^2}, \quad i = 1, \ldots, m.$$

TABLE 5.1
Profiles of Graduate Fellowship Applicants

| Applicants | GRE | GPA | College Rating | Recommendation Rating | Interview Rating |
|---|---|---|---|---|---|
| Alfred | 690 | 3.1 | 9 | 7 | 4 |
| Beverly | 590 | 3.9 | 7 | 6 | 10 |
| Calvin | 600 | 3.6 | 8 | 8 | 7 |
| Diane | 620 | 3.8 | 7 | 10 | 6 |
| Edward | 700 | 2.8 | 10 | 4 | 6 |
| Fran | 650 | 4.0 | 6 | 9 | 8 |

Similarly, the separation from the negative-ideal solution, $A^-$, is given by

$$S_i^- = \sqrt{\sum_{j=1}^{n} (v_{ij} - v_j^-)^2}, \quad i = 1, \ldots, m.$$

*Step 5. Calculate Similarities to Positive-Ideal Solution.*

$$C_i^* = S_i^- / (S_i^* + S_i^-), \quad i = 1, \ldots, m.$$

Note that $0 \leq C_i^* \leq 1$, where $C_i^* = 0$ when $A_i = A^-$, and $C_i^* = 1$ when $A_i = A^*$.

*Step 6. Rank Preference Order.* Choose an alternative with the maximum $C_i^*$ or rank alternatives according to $C_i^*$ in descending order.

*Case 5.1. Graduate Fellow Selection Decision.* A sociology department wants to select a student to receive a fellowship award from among applicants to its graduate program. The selection criteria of the department are GRE, GPA, college rating, recommendation rating, and faculty interview rating. Table 5.1 shows the evaluation of six applicants based on these attributes. The GRE score is on an 800-point scale, GPA on a 4.0 scale, and the three ratings are on a 10-point scale where 10 is the best. Suppose the department sets the importance weights for the five attributes as (0.3, 0.2, 0.2, 0.15, 0.15). Which of the candidates will receive the fellowship?

*Step 1. Normalization.* Since each attribute is measured on a different scale, an attribute normalization is required. The normalized ratings are given below:

$$
\begin{array}{c}
 \\
A \\
B \\
C \\
D \\
E \\
F
\end{array}
\begin{array}{ccccc}
X_1 & X_2 & X_3 & X_4 & X_5 \\
\left[\begin{array}{ccccc}
0.4381 & 0.3555 & 0.4623 & 0.3763 & 0.2306 \\
0.3746 & 0.4472 & 0.3596 & 0.3226 & 0.5764 \\
0.3809 & 0.4128 & 0.4109 & 0.4301 & 0.4035 \\
0.3936 & 0.4357 & 0.3596 & 0.5376 & 0.3458 \\
0.4444 & 0.3211 & 0.5137 & 0.2150 & 0.3458 \\
0.4127 & 0.4587 & 0.3082 & 0.4838 & 0.4611
\end{array}\right]
\end{array}
$$

where the first element $r_{11}$ was obtained from

$$0.4381 = 690/ \sqrt{(690^2 + 590^2 + \ldots + 650^2)} \ .$$

*Step 2. Weighted Normalization.* The chosen weights of (0.3, 0.2, 0.2, 0.15, 0.15) are multiplied with each column of the normalized rating matrix:

$$
\begin{array}{c}
A \\
B \\
C \\
D \\
E \\
F
\end{array}
\left[\begin{array}{ccccc}
0.1314 & 0.0711 & 0.0925 & 0.0564 & 0.0346^- \\
0.1124^- & 0.0894 & 0.0719 & 0.0484 & 0.0865^* \\
0.1143 & 0.0826 & 0.0822 & 0.0645 & 0.0605 \\
0.1181 & 0.0871 & 0.0719 & 0.0806^* & 0.0519 \\
0.1333^* & 0.0642^- & 0.1027^* & 0.0323^- & 0.0519 \\
0.1238 & 0.0917^* & 0.0616^- & 0.0726 & 0.0692
\end{array}\right]
$$

where the first element $v_{11}$ was calculated as $(0.1314 = 0.3 \times 0.4381)$.

*Step 3. Positive-Ideal and Negative-Ideal Solutions.* Since all the chosen attributes are of benefit (the higher, the more preference), the positive-ideal solution consists of the largest value of each column, which are denoted by the symbol "*" in Step 2. That is, $A^* = (0.1333, 0.0917, 0.1027, 0.0806, 0.0865)$.

The collection of the smallest values of each column in Step 2, which are denoted by the symbol "−," makes the negative-ideal solution. That is, $A^- = (0.1124, 0.0642, 0.0616, 0.0323, 0.0346)$.

*Step 4. Separation Measures.* The separation measures from $A^*$ are computed first:

$$S_A^* = \sqrt{\sum_{j=1}^{5} (v_{Aj} - v_j^*)^2}$$

$$= [(0.1314 - 0.1333)^2 + \ldots + (0.0346 - 0.0865)^2]^{\frac{1}{2}} = 0.0617$$

Separation measures from $A^*$ of all alternatives are

$$(S_A^*, S_B^*, S_C^*, S_D^*, S_E^*, S_F^*)$$

$$= (0.0617, 0.0493, 0.0424, 0.0490, 0.0655, 0.0463).$$

The separation measures from $A^-$ are computed as

$$S_A^- = \sqrt{\sum_{j=1}^{5} (v_{Aj} - v_j^-)^2}$$

$$= [(0.1314 - 0.1124)^2 + \ldots + (0.0346 - 0.0346)^2]^{\frac{1}{2}} = 0.0441$$

All separation measures from are

$$(S_A^-, S_B^-, S_C^-, S_D^-, S_E^-, S_F^-)$$

$$= (0.0441, 0.0608, 0.0498, 0.0575, 0.0493, 0.0609).$$

*Step 5. Similarities to Positive-Ideal Solution.* The value of $C_A^*$ is calculated from

$$C_A^* = S_A^- / (S_A^* + S_A^-)$$

$$= 0.0441 / (0.0617 + 0.0441) = 0.4167.$$

TABLE 5.2
Three Sets of Preference Rankings

| Applicants | $S^*$ | | $S^-$ | | $C^*$ | |
|---|---|---|---|---|---|---|
| | Value | Rank | Value | Rank | Value | Rank |
| A | 0.0617 | 5 | 0.0441 | 6 | 0.4167 | 6 |
| B | 0.0493 | 4 | 0.0608 | 2 | 0.5519 | 2 |
| C | 0.0424 | 1 | 0.0498 | 4 | 0.5396 | 4 |
| D | 0.0490 | 3 | 0.0575 | 3 | 0.5399 | 3 |
| E | 0.0655 | 6 | 0.0493 | 5 | 0.4291 | 5 |
| F | 0.0463 | 2 | 0.0609 | 1 | 0.5681 | 1 |

All similarities to the positive-ideal solution are

$$(C_A^*, C_B^*, C_C^*, C_D^*, C_E^*, C_F^*)$$

$$= (0.4167, 0.5519, 0.5396, 0.5399, 0.4291, 0.5681).$$

*Step 6. Preference Rank.* Based on the descending order of $C_i^*$, the preference order is given as [F, B, D, C, E, A], which selects applicant F as the awardee of the fellowship.

Three preference orders based on the positive-ideal ($S^*$), negative-ideal ($S^-$), and TOPSIS ($C^*$) are contrasted in Table 5.2. Applicant C is ranked first by $S^*$ and fourth by $S^-$. Applicant F is ranked second by $S^*$ and first by $S^-$. The selection of Applicant F by TOPSIS is equitable. The preference order by $C^*$ happens to be identical with that of $S^-$.

The choice behavior in TOPSIS can be explained by way of *indifference (value) curves*. A DM is assumed to give equal preference or value to any alternatives located on the same indifference curve. TOPSIS has a value function of $C^* = S^-/(S^* + S^-) = c$, where $c$ is a given value. The value function can be rewritten as $cS^* - (1 - c)S^- = 0$. This expression indicates a variation of a hyperbola where the difference of two weighted ($c$ and [1 $- c$]) distances from two fixed points (i.e., positive-ideal and negative-ideal points) is zero. Figure 5.2 shows some typical indifference curves in TOPSIS. Any curves with $c \geq 0.5$ are convex to the preference origin (i.e., positive-ideal point), which indicates the property of *diminishing marginal rate of substitution* observed in most indifference curves; whereas indifference curves with $c < 0.5$ are concave to the preference origin. This is an

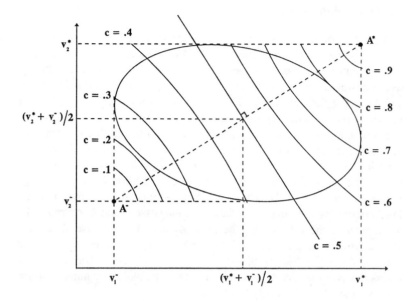

Figure 5.2.  Indifference Curves in TOPSIS
SOURCE: Hwang and Yoon (1981).

unusual case but it may be interpreted as a risk-prone attitude resulting from a pessimistic situation. When a DM recognizes one's solution is closer to the negative-ideal than to the positive-ideal, the DM is inclined to pick an alternative that consists of the best and worst attributes rather than one with two worse attributes. For example, one might want to get one A grade and one F grade rather than two D grades.

## 6. ELECTRE

The ELECTRE (Elimination et choix traduisant la réalité) method originated from Roy (1971) in the late 1960s. Since then Nijkamp and van Delft (1977) and Voogd (1983) have developed this method to its present state. The method dichotomizes preferred alternatives and nonpreferred ones by establishing outranking relationships. This method is most popular in Europe, especially among the French-speaking community.

## 6.1. Outranking Relationships

A greatly simplified car selection problem is employed to introduce the concept of an *outranking* relationship. A DM considers three cars based on two attributes: purchase price and gasoline efficiency. The three alternatives considered are $A_1$ = ($13,000, 18 MPG), $A_2$ = ($16,000, 21 MPG), and $A_3$ = ($18,000, 25 MPG). These alternatives nondominate each other because none of them excels the others in both attributes. Although we (as decision analysts) are not yet entitled to determine a preference between nondominated alternatives, a prior "likely preferred to" relationship might exist in the DM's mind. For instance, the DM is likely to prefer $A_1$ to $A_2$ because he or she does not want to pay an extra $3,000 for a gas mileage improvement of 3 MPG. Therefore, it is defined that $A_1$ outranks $A_2$. Furthermore, by the same token he or she may assess that $A_2$ outranks $A_3$. What then is the relationship between $A_1$ and $A_3$? Because these two alternatives are too separate, the DM may be hard put to assess a preference between them. Contrary to his or her previous judgments, the DM might assess that $A_3$ outranks $A_1$, which is quite acceptable, since human choice does not have to be logically transitive.

An outranking relationship can be concisely expressed by employing the binary relationship R. The notation $(A_p$ R $A_q)$ or $(A_p \rightarrow A_q)$ (more useful in a directed graph) means that $A_p$ outranks $A_q$. For example, the three assessments above are denoted as $(A_1$ R $A_2)$, $(A_2$ R $A_3)$, and $(A_3$ R $A_1)$. Formally, an outranking relationship of $(A_p$ R $A_q)$ states that even though two alternatives $A_p$ and $A_q$ do not dominate each other, it is realistic to accept the risk of regarding $A_p$ as almost surely better than $A_q$. Accordingly, the outranking relationship R is not required to be transitive. That is, $(A_1$ R $A_2)$ and $(A_2$ R $A_3)$ do not necessarily imply $(A_1$ R $A_3)$. Such an outranking relationship is both ambiguous and practical. The outranking relationship in ELECTRE, however, is determined in an objective fashion by simultaneously employing concordance and discordance indexes.

## 6.2. Preferred Alternatives

Because the outranking relationship is not transitive, we may not eliminate $A_q$ at once even when we have a relationship of $(A_p$ R $A_q)$ or $(A_p \rightarrow A_q)$. We should consider all R relationships in a given problem and eliminate nonpreferred alternatives based on the overall dominance structure. For example, nine outranking relationships from eight alternatives are

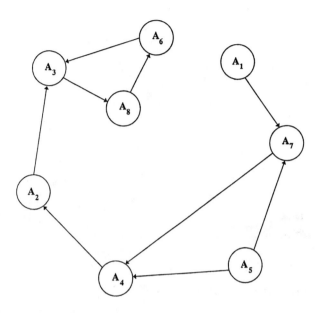

Figure 6.1. A Digraph for Eight Alternatives

given: $(A_1 \rightarrow A_7)$, $(A_2 \rightarrow A_3)$, $(A_3 \rightarrow A_8)$, $(A_4 \rightarrow A_2)$, $(A_5 \rightarrow A_4)$, $(A_5 \rightarrow A_7)$, $(A_6 \rightarrow A_3)$, $(A_7 \rightarrow A_4)$, and $(A_8 \rightarrow A_6)$. Figure 6.1 shows a digraph that represents the above nine outranking relationships all together. In this digraph each node represents an alternative. When a directed path begins in a node and comes back to this very node, we call the path a cycle. All nodes in a cycle are considered to have an equivalent preference. We then construct an acyclic digraph by combining the nodes in a cycle into a single node. We notice a cycle of $A_3 \rightarrow A_8 \rightarrow A_6 \rightarrow A_3$ in Figure 6.1.

The kernel (or core) of an acyclic digraph is a reduced set of nodes that is preferred to the set of nodes that do not belong to the kernel. In other words the kernel is a set of preferred alternatives defined by ELECTRE. The kernel K should satisfy the following two conditions:

1. Each node in K is not outranked by any other node in K.
2. Every node *not* in K is outranked by at least one node in K.

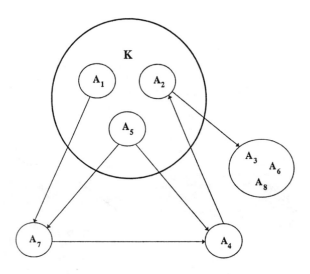

Figure 6.2. The Kernel of Figure 6.1

The digraph shown in Figure 6.1 is considered to illustrate the kernel identification process. First, we choose any nodes that have no entering arrows; these are $A_1$ and $A_5$. Then we add any alternatives that satisfy the above conditions. Only alternative $A_2$ can be added. Figure 6.2 shows the kernel of eight alternatives. The set of preferred alternatives defined by the kernel is $K = \{A_1, A_2, A_5\}$.

## 6.3. ELECTRE

The ELECTRE method formulates concordance and discordance indexes in order to obtain outranking relationships, then renders a set of preferred alternatives by forming a kernel. Concordance and discordance indexes can be viewed as measurements of satisfaction and dissatisfaction that a DM feels on choosing one alternative over the other. The method is illustrated by the following case.

*Case 6.1. Budget Reduction Decision for Athletic Programs.* This case was described in detail in Chapter 1, and its decision matrix was presented in Table 1.1. The "miscellaneous impact" attribute utilized a five-point scale ranging from *very low* (5) to *very high* (1) with *very low* being the best.

*Step 1. Normalization.* Attributes $X_2$ and $X_3$ are of benefit criterion (the more, the better) but attribute $X_1$ is of cost. Therefore, the values of $X_1$ (30, 29, 12) are inverted (1/30, 1/29, 1/12) in order to transform this attribute to a benefit one. Since each attribute has different measurement scales, a normalization is necessary to make their values comparable. The comparable ratings by vector normalization are given below:

$$
\begin{array}{c}
\quad\quad X_1 \quad\quad X_2 \quad\quad X_3 \\
\begin{array}{c} A_1 \\ A_2 \\ A_3 \end{array}
\begin{bmatrix}
0.3466 & 0.9126 & 0.4243 \\
0.3587 & 0.3914 & 0.5657 \\
0.8667 & 0.1179 & 0.7071
\end{bmatrix}
\end{array}
$$

where element $r_{21} = 0.3587$ was obtained from

$$
(1/29)/\sqrt{(1/30)^2 + (1/29)^2 + (1/12)^2} \; ,
$$

and $r_{33} = 0.7071$ was from $5/\sqrt{3^2 + 4^2 + 5^2}$.

*Step 2. Weighted Normalization.* The set of attribute weights for the Athletic Department problem were developed using the personal assessments of the department leaders. The number of people directly affected by dropping each sport was given a weight of 20%. The most important category, Athletic Department money saved, was weighted at 70%. The third attribute, miscellaneous, was weighted at 10%. These weights $(w_1, w_2, w_3) = (0.2, 0.7, 0.1)$ are multiplied with each column of the normalized rating matrix. The weighted normalized ratings $v_{ij}$ are computed as

$$
\begin{array}{c}
\quad\quad X_1 \quad\quad X_2 \quad\quad X_3 \\
\begin{array}{c} A_1 \\ A_2 \\ A_3 \end{array}
\begin{bmatrix}
0.0693 & 0.6388 & 0.0424 \\
0.0717 & 0.2740 & 0.0566 \\
0.1733 & 0.0825 & 0.0707
\end{bmatrix}
\end{array}
$$

*Step 3. Concordance and Discordance Sets.* For each pair of alternatives $A_p$ and $A_q$ ($p, q = 1, 2, \ldots, m$ and $p \neq q$), the set of attributes is divided into two distinct subsets. The concordance set, which is composed of all attributes for which alternative $A_p$ is preferred to alternative $A_q$, can be written as

$$C(p, q) = \left\{ j \mid v_{pj} \geq v_{qj} \right\}$$

where $v_{pj}$ is the weighted normalized rating of alternative $A_p$ with respect to the $j$th attribute. In other words, $C(p, q)$ is the collection of attributes where $A_p$ is better than or equal to $A_q$.

The complement of $C(p, q)$, which is called the discordance set, contains all attributes for which $A_p$ is worse than $A_q$. This can be written as

$$D(p, q) = \left\{ j \mid v_{pj} < v_{qj} \right\}.$$

Note that $C(p, q)$ is not equal to $D(q, p)$ when tied ratings exist.

The concordance and discordance sets for the Athletic Department problem are obtained as

$$C(1, 2) = \{2\} \qquad D(1, 2) = \{1, 3\}$$

$$C(1, 3) = \{2\} \qquad D(1, 3) = \{1, 3\}$$

$$C(2, 1) = \{1, 3\} \qquad D(2, 1) = \{2\}$$

$$C(2, 3) = \{2\} \qquad D(2, 3) = \{1, 3\}$$

$$C(3, 1) = \{1, 3\} \qquad D(3, 1) = \{2\}$$

$$C(3, 2) = \{1, 3\} \qquad D(3, 2) = \{2\}.$$

*Step 4. Concordance and Discordance Indexes.* The relative power of each concordance set is measured by means of the concordance index. The concordance index $C_{pq}$ represents the degree of confidence in the pairwise judgments of $(A_p \rightarrow A_q)$. The concordance index of $C(p, q)$ is defined as

$$C_{pq} = \sum_{j*} w_{j*}$$

where $j*$ are attributes contained in the concordance set $C(p, q)$.

The discordance index, on the other hand, measures the power of $D(p, q)$. The discordance index of $D(p, q)$, which represents the degree of disagreement in $(A_p \rightarrow A_q)$, can be defined as

$$D_{pq} = (\sum_{j^\circ} |v_{pj^\circ} - v_{qj^\circ}|)/(\sum_j |v_{pj} - v_{qj}|)$$

where $j^\circ$ are attributes that are contained in the discordance set $D(p, q)$.

For the given problem, a concordance index $C_{21}$ is obtained as follows: Since $C(2, 1) = \{1, 3\}$, $C_{21} = \sum w_j^* = w_1 + w_3 = 0.2 + 0.1 = 0.3$. A discordance index $D_{21}$ is calculated as follows: Since $D(2, 1) = \{2\}$, the formula for $D_{21}$ takes the form:

$$D_{21} = (\sum |v_{22} - v_{12}|)/(\sum_{j=1}^{3} |v_{2j} - v_{1j}|) = 0.9565.$$

The complete list of concordance and discordance indexes is as follows:

$C_{12} = 0.7 \qquad D_{12} = 0.0435$

$C_{13} = 0.7 \qquad D_{13} = 0.1921$

$C_{21} = 0.3 \qquad D_{21} = 0.9565$

$C_{23} = 0.7 \qquad D_{23} = 0.3766$

$C_{31} = 0.3 \qquad D_{31} = 0.8079$

$C_{32} = 0.3 \qquad D_{32} = 0.6234.$

*Step 5. Outranking Relationships.* The dominance relationship of alternative $A_p$ over alternative $A_q$ becomes stronger with a higher concordance index $C_{pq}$ and a lower discordance index $D_{pq}$. The method defines that $A_p$ outranks $A_q$ when $C_{pq} \geq \overline{C}$ and $D_{pq} < \overline{D}$, where $\overline{C}$ and $\overline{D}$ are the averages of $C_{pq}$ and $D_{pq}$, respectively.

For the given problem, $\overline{C} = (0.7 + 0.7 + \ldots + 0.3)/6 = 0.5$ and $\overline{D} = (0.0435 + 0.1921 + \ldots + 0.6234)/6 = 0.5$.

TABLE 6.1
Determination of Outranking Relationship

| $C_{pq}$ | Is $(C_{pq} \geq \overline{C})$? | $D_{pq}$ | Is $(D_{pq} < \overline{D})$? | Is $(A_p \rightarrow A_q)$? |
|---|---|---|---|---|
| $C_{12}$ | Yes | $D_{12}$ | Yes | Yes |
| $C_{13}$ | Yes | $D_{13}$ | Yes | Yes |
| $C_{21}$ | No | $D_{21}$ | No | No |
| $C_{23}$ | Yes | $D_{23}$ | Yes | Yes |
| $C_{31}$ | No | $D_{31}$ | No | No |
| $C_{32}$ | No | $D_{32}$ | No | No |

Table 6.1 illustrates the determination of outranking relationships. Three outranking relationships are obtained: $(A_1 \rightarrow A_2)$, $(A_1 \rightarrow A_3)$, and $(A_2 \rightarrow A_3)$. Only alternative $A_1$ remains in the kernel, which makes $A_1$ the optimal choice. The Athletic Department did in fact eliminate the ski program (i.e., $A_1$), for which it received harsh criticism. However, by ELECTRE analysis we determined that dropping the ski program was indeed the best choice and that criticism of the Athletic Department was unfounded.

### 6.4. Complementary Analysis

A weakness of ELECTRE might lie in its use of the critical threshold values $\overline{C}$ and $\overline{D}$. These values are rather arbitrary, although their impact upon the ultimate result may be significant. We also notice that ELECTRE does not indicate a preference among nodes (alternatives) in the kernel K. The net outranking relationship is introduced to address these problems. First, complementary ELECTRE defines the net concordance index $C_p$, which measures the degree to which the dominance of alternative $A_p$ over competing alternatives exceeds the dominance of competing alternatives over $A_p$. Similarly, the net discordance index $D_p$ measures the relative weakness of alternative $A_p$ with respect to other alternatives. These net indexes are mathematically denoted as

$$C_p = \sum_{\substack{k=1 \\ k \neq p}}^{m} C_{pk} - \sum_{\substack{k=1 \\ k \neq p}}^{m} C_{kp}$$

$$D_p = \sum_{\substack{k=1 \\ k \neq p}}^{m} D_{pk} - \sum_{\substack{k=1 \\ k \neq p}}^{m} D_{kp}.$$

Obviously, an alternative $A_p$ has a greater preference with a higher $C_p$ and a lower $D_p$. Hence the final selection should satisfy the condition that its net concordance index should be at a maximum and its net discordance index at a minimum. If both these conditions are not satisfied, the alternative that scores the highest average rank can be selected as the final solution.

For the Athletic Department problem, the net concordance and discordance indexes are

$C_1 = 0.8$         $D_1 = -1.53$

$C_2 = 0.0$         $D_2 = 0.67$

$C_3 = -0.8$       $D_3 = 0.86$

where, for example, they are calculated by

$$C_1 = (C_{12} + C_{13}) - (C_{21} + C_{31}) = 0.8$$

$$D_3 = (D_{31} + D_{32}) - (D_{13} + D_{23}) = 0.86.$$

The preference ranks based on the net concordance index and the net discordance index in this case are identical: $[A_1, A_2, A_3]$ where $A_1$ is the first rank and $A_3$ is the last.

# 7. METHODS FOR QUALITATIVE DATA

Qualitative data can be easily transformed to either rank data or pairwise comparison data. This chapter presents two methods that work with qualitative data: the Median Ranking method, which accepts rank (ordinal) data, and the AHP method, which accepts pairwise comparison data.

TABLE 7.1
Qualitative Data for Three Cars

| Cars | Prestige | Appeal | Safety | Reliability |
|------|----------|--------|--------|-------------|
| $A_1$ | Good | Excellent | Fair | Good |
| $A_2$ | Excellent | Good | Very Good | Fair |
| $A_3$ | Very Good | Very Good | Good | Very Good |

## 7.1. Median Ranking Method

Consider an automobile evaluation problem. The decision matrix, which exhibits three full-size cars based on four qualitative attributes, is shown in Table 7.1. From this matrix we can easily obtain the following four ranks from each attribute (called attributewise ranks):

| | $X_1$ | $X_2$ | $X_3$ | $X_4$ | Total |
|--|-------|-------|-------|-------|-------|
| $A_1$ | 3 | 1 | 3 | 2 | 9 |
| $A_2$ | 1 | 3 | 1 | 3 | 8 |
| $A_3$ | 2 | 2 | 2 | 1 | 7 |

where $A_2$ is the first, $A_3$ the second, and $A_1$ the third rank with respect to attribute $X_1$.

When the DM assigns equal importance among all the attributes, the simplest way to obtain an overall ranking is to add the four attributewise ranks and rank them in ascending order. The ranking is then $[A_3, A_2, A_1]$ where $A_3$ is the first and $A_1$ is the last. However, this approach may not be valid because the ordinal scale does not allow any arithmetic operations.

We observe that the four attributewise ranks conflict with each other. For example, attribute $X_1$ picks $A_2$ as the first rank and $A_1$ as the last rank, whereas attribute $X_2$ picks $A_1$ as the first and $A_2$ as the last. However, the DM needs a consensus from the four different attributewise ranks. One way of obtaining a consensus ranking is to create a rank that differs from all attributewise ranks as little as possible. Cook and Seiford (1978) introduced a distance function as a measure of agreement or disagreement between rankings. The disagreement (indicator) for an alternative $A_i$ to become the $k$th overall rank is defined as the sum of distances between the attributewise rank and the $k$th rank. That is,

$$d_{ik} = \sum_{j=1}^{n} |s_{ij} - k|$$

where $s_{ij}$ is the attributewise rank of $A_i$ according to the $j$th attribute. For example, $d_{11}$, which is the total distance for $A_1$ to be ranked first, is determined by

$$d_{11} = \sum_{j=1}^{4} |s_{1j} - 1|$$

$$= |3 - 1| + |1 - 1| + |3 - 1| + |2 - 1| = 5.$$

Similarly, $d_{12} = \sum_{j=1}^{4} |s_{1j} - 2| = 3$ and $d_{33} = \sum_{j=1}^{4} |s_{3j} - 3| = 5$. We can compute all 9 ($= 3 \times 3$) total distances and present them in a distance matrix as follows:

$$
\begin{array}{c}
 \\
A_1 \\
A_2 \\
A_3
\end{array}
\begin{array}{ccc}
\text{1st} & \text{2nd} & \text{3rd} \\
\left[\begin{array}{ccc}
5 & 3 & 3 \\
4 & 4 & 4 \\
3 & 1 & 5
\end{array}\right]
\end{array}
$$

Now we should pick three elements in the distance matrix to assign ranks to each alternative; that is, choose three (the number of alternatives in the problem) elements in the different rows and columns whose sum is the minimum. This can be accomplished by using the so-called "Hungarian Method" (Kuhn, 1955) of linear programming. The Hungarian method takes the following solution steps:

*Step 1. Row Reduction.* Choose the smallest element in each row and subtract this amount from all elements in the row. Repeat this process for all rows.

*Step 2. Column Reduction.* Choose the smallest element in each column and then subtract this amount from all elements in the column. Repeat this process for all columns.

*Step 3. Cover the Zeros.* Draw the fewest horizontal or vertical lines that will cover all "zero" elements in the matrix. When the minimum number of lines required to cover all zero elements is equal to the number of rows (or columns) in the matrix, an optimal assignment among the zero elements can be found. For the selection procedure go to Step 5. If the number of lines is fewer than the number of rows (or columns), go to Step 4.

*Step 4. Create New Zeros.* Begin with the matrix and lines from Step 3. Find the smallest uncovered element (not covered by a line) and subtract it from all uncovered elements, including itself; add it to all elements at the line intersections. Erase all horizontal lines and vertical lines and return to Step 3.

*Step 5. Make Assignment.* Examine rows successively, beginning with row 1, for a row with exactly one zero. If one exists, mark this zero with the symbol $\Delta$ to denote an assignment. Cross out (X) the other zeros in the same column so additional assignments will not be made to that column. Repeat the process until each row has no unmarked zeros.

The Hungarian algorithm is now applied to the car evaluation problem. The solution steps are illustrated in Figure 7.1. The superscripts in the final matrix indicate the sequence of operations in Step 5. The solution indicates that $A_2$ is the first, $A_3$ is the second, and $A_1$ is the third overall rank. Note that this ranking differs from that made by the sum of attributes ranking.

Two extensions can be made for the construction of a distance matrix:

1. So far we have assumed that each attribute has equal importance. If they have different weights $w_j$, the total distance can be modified as $d_{ik} = \sum_j w_j |s_{ij} - k|$.
2. When a tie occurs in the attributewise rank, an average rank is assigned to the tied alternatives. For example, when two alternatives are tied for the first rank, a rank of 1.5 $[= (1 + 2)/2]$ should be assigned.

*Case 7.1. Host State Selection for Radioactive Waste Management Facility.* At its December 8, 1987, meeting in Kansas City, Missouri, the Central Interstate Low-Level Radioactive Waste Compact Commission (hereafter called the "Commission") directed US Ecology, Inc., to recommend a state to host the compact region's first low-level radioactive waste management facility (Paton & Bradbury, 1987). Specifically the scope of the Commission's request to US Ecology was as follows:

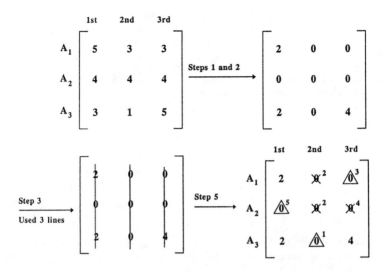

Figure 7.1. Illustration of the Hungarian Method

1. Recommend which of the five compact states (Arkansas, Kansas, Louisiana, Nebraska, or Oklahoma) should be selected to serve as the first Host State for locating a low-level radioactive waste management facility.
2. Base the recommendations on three key factors (i.e., attributes):
   - Environmental considerations, including those aspects related to the physical characteristics of an area necessary to meet the siting requirement imposed by the Nuclear Regulatory Commission.
   - Waste generation considerations, identifying the waste classification and activity levels in addition to the gross disposal volume of each compact state.
   - Transportation considerations, including the various aspects associated with transporting radioactive wastes from the several generators to the waste management facility.
3. Support the recommendation with a narrative evaluation based on existing data with due regard for the Commission's previous actions, and without any attempt to "quantify" differences among the states or rely upon a rigorous mathematical formula or similar quantitative assessment concepts.

TABLE 7.2
Data for Waste Management Site Selection

| (Weight) | $X_1$ (Highest) | $X_2$ (Moderate) | $X_3$ (Lowest) |
|---|---|---|---|
| States (Grouped from most favorable to least favorable) | • Nebraska/ Kansas | • Nebraska/ Louisiana | • Arkansas |
| | • Oklahoma/ Arkansas/ Louisiana | • Arkansas | • Oklahoma/ Kansas |
| | | • Kansas/ Oklahoma | • Nebraska/ Louisiana |

NOTE: $X_1$ = environment, $X_2$ = waste generation, $X_3$ = transportation.
SOURCE: Paton and Bradbury (1987).

As requested by the Commission, US Ecology made a qualitative evaluation based on three attributes as shown in Table 7.2. As can be seen, Arkansas, Kansas, Louisiana, and Nebraska rank high in at least one category. Nebraska shares highest place for both of the two highest weighted factors and ranks low for the third (lowest weighted). The two states ranked along with Nebraska for the high weighted factors are Louisiana for waste generation, and Kansas for environmental consideration. However, neither Kansas nor Louisiana rate high for more than one of the three factors. Similarly, although Arkansas rates high for transportation considerations (lowest weighted), it ranks low for the other two factors. Oklahoma does not rate high for any of the three factors. Therefore, US Ecology recommended that the first host state be Nebraska.

Since US Ecology arrived at their conclusion in an informal way (i.e., without the use of a formal MADM technique), we apply the Median Ranking method to the waste management siting problem. The attributewise rankings generated from Table 7.2 are

| State | $X_1$ | $X_2$ | $X_3$ |
|---|---|---|---|
| (A)rkansas | 4 | 3 | 1 |
| (K)ansas | 1.5 | 4.5 | 2.5 |
| (L)ousiana | 4 | 1.5 | 4.5 |
| (N)ebraska | 1.5 | 1.5 | 4.5 |
| (O)klahoma | 4 | 4.5 | 2.5 |

A mean ranking was assigned in many places because of the occurrence of ties. For example, because Nebraska and Kansas are tied in first place for attribute $X_1$, a mean rank of 1.5 [$= (1 + 2)/2$] is given to both states. Assume that equal weights are given to all three attributes. The distance matrix is then constructed:

|   | 1st | 2nd | 3rd | 4th | 5th |
|---|-----|-----|-----|-----|-----|
| A | 5   | 4   | 3   | 4   | 7   |
| K | 5.5 | 3.5 | 3.5 | 4.5 | 6.5 |
| L | 7   | 5   | 4   | 3   | 5   |
| N | 4.5 | 3.5 | 4.5 | 5.5 | 7.5 |
| O | 8   | 5   | 3   | 2   | 4   |

The Hungarian algorithm renders two ranks: [N, K, A, L, O] and [N, K, A, O, L] where N(ebraska) is the first choice, K is the next, and L and O are tied for the fourth rank. This result matches with that of US Ecology. It may not be necessary to perform another analysis with unequal weights, because it is obvious that the solution with highest weight on $X_1$ and moderate weight on $X_2$, where Nebraska received highest ranks, will pick Nebraska again.

Actually the Median Ranking method is adapted from a group decision making technique (Hwang & Lin, 1987). Cook and Seiford (1978) considered the problems of combining the ordinal preferences of $n$ persons in order to form a consensus. Here we combine $n$ attributewise ranks to form a consensus ranking. This approach is called the Median Ranking method because the overall ranking differs as little as possible from all available attributewise ranks.

## 7.2. AHP: Hierarchical SAW Method

The analytic hierarchy process (AHP), developed by Saaty (1980), is essentially the formalization of our intuitive understanding of a complex problem using a hierarchical structure. The crux of the AHP is to enable a DM to structure a MADM problem visually in the form of an attribute hierarchy. A hierarchy has at least three levels: focus or overall goal of the problem at the top, multiple criteria that define alternatives in the middle, and competing alternatives at the bottom. When criteria are highly abstract,

60

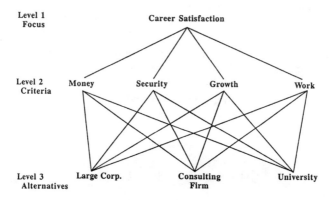

Figure 7.2. A Hierarchy for Career Choice Satisfaction

such as "well being," subcriteria (or sub-subcriteria) are generated sequentially through a multilevel hierarchy.

For example, consider the problem of an accountant (female) who needs to decide among three career alternatives: $(A_1)$ partner in a large corporation, $(A_2)$ her own consulting firm, and $(A_3)$ faculty position at a university. Figure 7.2 shows how the accountant generated decision criteria by means of a hierarchical structure. At level 1, the focus is overall job satisfaction. Level 2 comprises the criteria that contribute to job satisfaction: Money $(M)$, Job security $(S)$, Growth $(G)$, and Work environment $(W)$. Level 3 consists of the three job possibilities: $A_1$, $A_2$, and $A_3$.

It is obvious that each criterion in level 2 should contribute differently to her job satisfaction. She decides on the relative importance among four criteria by pairwise comparisons because pairwise comparisons are much easier to make than a comparison of four criteria simultaneously.

In order to help a DM assess the pairwise comparisons, Saaty created a nine-point intensity scale of importance between two elements. The suggested numbers to express degrees of preference between the two elements A and B are shown in Table 7.3. Intermediate values (2, 4, 6 and 8) can be used to represent compromises between the preferences.

In the career choice problem, there are four criteria in level 2. The accountant then makes six pairwise judgments among four criteria with respect to level 1, career satisfaction: $(M : S) = (7 : 1)$, $(M : G) = (1 : 1)$, $(M : W) = (7 : 1)$, $(S : G) = (1 : 3)$, $(S : W) = (2 : 1)$, $(G : W) = (5 : 1)$. This

| if A is . . .<br>. . . as (than) B | then the preference number<br>to assign is |
|---|---|
| equally important | 1 |
| moderately more important | 3 |
| strongly more important | 5 |
| very strongly more important | 7 |
| extremely more important | 9 |

SOURCE: Adapted from Saaty (1980).

information can be concisely contained in a matrix whose element at row $i$ and column $j$ is the ratio of row $i$ and column $j$. That is,

$$
\begin{array}{c}
\begin{array}{cccc} M & S & G & W \end{array} \\
\begin{array}{c} M \\ S \\ G \\ W \end{array}
\begin{bmatrix}
1 & M/S & M/G & M/W \\
S/M & 1 & S/G & S/W \\
G/M & G/S & 1 & G/W \\
W/M & W/S & W/G & 1
\end{bmatrix}
\end{array}
=
\begin{array}{c}
\begin{array}{cccc} M & S & G & W \end{array} \\
\begin{array}{c} M \\ S \\ G \\ W \end{array}
\begin{bmatrix}
1 & 7 & 1 & 7 \\
1/7 & 1 & 1/3 & 2 \\
1 & 3 & 1 & 5 \\
1/7 & 1/2 & 1/5 & 1
\end{bmatrix}
\end{array}
$$

Next she makes pairwise comparisons of three job contributions in level 3 with respect to four criteria in level 2:

$$
\begin{array}{c}
\text{for } M \begin{array}{ccc} A_1 & A_2 & A_3 \end{array} \\
\begin{array}{c} A_1 \\ A_2 \\ A_3 \end{array}
\begin{bmatrix}
1 & 1/3 & 2 \\
3 & 1 & 5 \\
1/2 & 1/5 & 1
\end{bmatrix}
\end{array}
\qquad
\begin{array}{c}
\text{for } S \begin{array}{ccc} A_1 & A_2 & A_3 \end{array} \\
\begin{array}{c} A_1 \\ A_2 \\ A_3 \end{array}
\begin{bmatrix}
1 & 3 & 1/5 \\
1/3 & 1 & 1/7 \\
5 & 7 & 1
\end{bmatrix}
\end{array}
$$

$$
\begin{array}{c}
\text{for } G \begin{array}{ccc} A_1 & A_2 & A_3 \end{array} \\
\begin{array}{c} A_1 \\ A_2 \\ A_3 \end{array}
\begin{bmatrix}
1 & 1/5 & 2 \\
5 & 1 & 7 \\
1/2 & 1/7 & 1
\end{bmatrix}
\end{array}
\qquad
\begin{array}{c}
\text{for } W \begin{array}{ccc} A_1 & A_2 & A_3 \end{array} \\
\begin{array}{c} A_1 \\ A_2 \\ A_3 \end{array}
\begin{bmatrix}
1 & 1/3 & 1/5 \\
3 & 1 & 1/3 \\
5 & 3 & 1
\end{bmatrix}
\end{array}
$$

After the construction of the pairwise comparison matrix, the next step is to retrieve the weights of each element in the matrix. For an approximation method that provides sufficiently close results in most situations, Saaty suggested the geometric mean of a row (See Section 2.2.2): (a) Multiply the $n$ elements in each row, take the $n$th root, and prepare a new column for the resulting numbers, then (b) normalize the new column (i.e., divide each number by the sum of the numbers). The weights of the four criteria are computed as shown below:

$$
\begin{array}{c}
\textit{Geometric Mean} \\
\begin{array}{c} M \\ S \\ G \\ W \end{array}
\begin{bmatrix}
(1 \times 7 \times 1 \times 7)^{\frac{1}{4}} = 2.65 \\
(1/7 \times 1 \times 1/3 \times 2)^{\frac{1}{4}} = 0.56 \\
(1 \times 3 \times 1 \times 5)^{\frac{1}{4}} = 1.97 \\
(1/7 \times 1/2 \times 1/5 \times 1)^{\frac{1}{4}} = 0.35
\end{bmatrix}
=
\begin{bmatrix}
0.48 \\ 0.10 \\ 0.36 \\ 0.06
\end{bmatrix} \\
\text{sum} \quad 5.53 \qquad\qquad\qquad 1.00
\end{array}
$$

Similarly, the relative contributions (i.e., weights) among three jobs toward the four criteria are computed below:

$$
\begin{array}{c}
\begin{array}{cccc} \ \ M & \ \ S & \ \ G & \ \ W \end{array} \\
\begin{array}{c} A_1 \\ A_2 \\ A_3 \end{array}
\begin{bmatrix}
0.23 & 0.19 & 0.17 & 0.10 \\
0.65 & 0.08 & 0.74 & 0.26 \\
0.12 & 0.73 & 0.09 & 0.64
\end{bmatrix}
\end{array}
$$

The final stage of the AHP is to compute the contribution of each alternative to the overall goal (i.e., job satisfaction) by aggregating the resulting weights vertically. The overall priority for each alternative is obtained by summing the product of the criteria weight and the contribution of the alternative, with respect to that criterion. Refer to Figure 7.3 for the career choice problem. The computation of the overall priority for alternative $A_1$ is as follows: $0.48(0.23) + 0.10(0.19) + 0.36(0.17) + 0.06(0.10) = 0.1966$. Similarly, they are 0.6020 and 0.2014 for $A_2$ and $A_3$ respectively. Therefore, her choice is to have her own accounting firm ($A_2$).

*Case 7.2. The Iran Hostage Rescue Decision.* A shroud of secrecy surrounds the facts pertaining to how the decision for the Iran hostage rescue attempt of April 28, 1980, was made. An American air rescue team

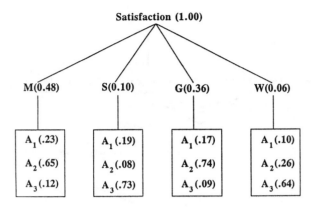

Figure 7.3. Priorities for Each Hierarchial Level

was sent to bring out 53 American hostages from Teheran where they had been held captive since early November, 1979. Saaty, Vargas, and Barzilay (1982) applied the AHP to simulate the decision process faced by President Carter.

The mission was a complicated plan involving troops, airplanes, helicopters, a long flight, a landing in the desert, transferring overland to Teheran, taking out the hostages, and returning to safety. Undoubtedly the likelihood of success of a rescue operation is a compelling factor in deciding whether to go or not to go ahead with it. It is crucial to know how military experts involved in national security matters have defined success for such a mission. High success means no hostage or military deaths, medium success means a few military and no hostage deaths, and low success means a few military and a few hostage deaths.

Because it is obvious that President Carter would send the troops under a likelihood of high success and would not under a likelihood of low success, Saaty et al. surmised that a likelihood of medium success was presented to the President, who needed justification for his action. He then made his go/no-go decision, and how he might have done this is what we want to examine.

The hierarchical structure for the hostage rescue mission is shown in Figure 7.4. It was assumed that the main factors that could have played an important role in President Carter's mind are

Figure 7.4. A Hierarchy for the Hostage Rescue Mission
SOURCE: Adapted from Saaty, Vargas, and Barzilay (1982).

- Hostages' lives: The President as well as every American wished the safe return of all 53 hostages.
- President Carter's political life: The President's concern about the influence of the decision on his chances for re-election.
- Military costs: The President's concern about the loss of soldier's lives in the operation.
- U.S. prestige: The President's concern about the effect of the decision on relations with foreign states and the image of strength/weakness projected by the United States.

To analyze the President's go/no-go decision, we start by comparing the factors of level 3 as to their contribution to the hostage rescue mission in the light of the presumed likelihood of medium success. Thus it was asked: Given two factors, which one is more important in the context of a likelihood of medium success to make the final decision, and how much more important? These judgments were obtained from experts close to the scene at the time and also from available public sources. Table 7.4 shows, for example, that the hostages' lives had *strong* dominance over military costs in the President's mind. Thus the value five is assigned in the first

TABLE 7.4
Relative Weights of the Factors Toward Rescue Mission

| | A | B | C | D | Weights |
|---|---|---|---|---|---|
| A. Hostages' lives | 1 | 1/3 | 5 | 1/3 | .15 |
| B. Carter's political life | 3 | 1 | 7 | 4 | .54 |
| C. Military costs | 1/5 | 1/7 | 1 | 1/6 | .05 |
| D. U.S. Prestige | 3 | 1/4 | 6 | 1 | .26 |

SOURCE: Saaty, Vargas, and Barzilay (1982).

row and third column position and its reciprocal value in the first column and third row position. As can be seen from the column of priorities in Table 7.4, the most important factor is Carter's political life.

For each factor we considered the question: Which alternative (go/no-go) is more favorable considering only that "factor" under a likelihood of medium success? The results are shown in Table 7.5. Thus, for example, when considering hostages' lives only and with a likelihood of medium success, the go/no-go decision was equally important.

To compose the factors' weights with those of the go/no-go alternatives, we multiply the weight of the factors by the priorities of the alternatives under each factor. Multiplication of two matrices makes this easy to comprehend:

$$
\begin{array}{c}
\\
\text{Go} \\
\text{No–go}
\end{array}
\begin{array}{cccc}
A & B & C & D \\
\end{array}
\begin{bmatrix}
0.5 & 0.75 & 0.125 & 0.8 \\
0.5 & 0.25 & 0.875 & 0.2
\end{bmatrix}
\begin{array}{c}
A \\
B \\
C \\
D
\end{array}
\begin{bmatrix}
0.15 \\
0.54 \\
0.05 \\
0.26
\end{bmatrix}
=
\begin{array}{c}
\text{Go} \\
\text{No–go}
\end{array}
\begin{bmatrix}
0.69 \\
0.31
\end{bmatrix}
$$

The result shows that the contribution of Go toward the mission is much larger than that of No-go. Thus his decision to send a rescue team can be justified.

The practical nature of the AHP method has led to its application in highly diverse areas including education, politics, and sociology. See Zahedi (1986) for an application review. The close relationship between the AHP and the SAW method (Chapter 4) was first noted by Hwang and Yoon (1981). They called the AHP the hierarchical SAW because the hierarchical levels in AHP are connected by algebraic addition.

TABLE 7.5
Go/No-go Priorities Toward Four Attributes

| For A | Go | No-go | Priorities | For B | Go | No-go | Priorities |
|-------|----|-------|------------|-------|----|-------|------------|
| Go | 1 | 1 | .5 | Go | 1 | 3 | .75 |
| No-go | 1 | 1 | .5 | No-go | 1/3 | 1 | .25 |

| For C | Go | No-go | Priorities | For D | Go | No-go | Priorities |
|-------|----|-------|------------|-------|----|-------|------------|
| Go | 1 | 1/7 | .125 | Go | 1 | 4 | .8 |
| No-go | 7 | 1 | .875 | No-go | 1/4 | 1 | .2 |

SOURCE: Saaty, Vargas, and Barzilay (1982).

# 8. EXTENSIONS

## 8.1. Soft Data Implementation

There are various ways for a DM to make estimations or describe observations. Table 8.1 illustrates three common ways: fuzzy, imprecise, and certain (point). We understand the difficulty or cognitive requirement in describing an object by a point description. For instance, who can precisely predict the next year's inflation rate as a point estimate? For this reason a DM prefers to use a fuzzy or imprecise description (e.g., about 4% or 3.5%-4.5%) rather than a certain one (e.g., exactly 3.8%). Certain descriptions are often referred to as *hard* data whereas other forms of data are generally referred to as *soft* data. The certain estimate is a very special kind of data description method, to be used only in ideal situations, whereas soft estimates can easily be applied to real situations.

However, most MADM methods permit only certain data input and therefore cannot be implemented in a soft data environment. Therefore, we need new mathematical operations and prioritization rules for the implementation of soft data.

Imprecise data of (3.5%-4.5%) can be changed to an error data type such as (4 ± 0.5)%. The Propagation of Errors technique (Pugh & Winslow, 1966; Yoon, 1990) was utilized to measure the aggregated error in alternative values due to errors in attribute rating and weight. The SAW method with imprecise data was studied by Yoon and Kim (1989). See Yoon (1989) for the AHP with imprecise data.

TABLE 8.1
Different Ways to Describe Observations

| Observations | Description | | |
| --- | --- | --- | --- |
| | *Fuzzy* | *Imprecise* | *Certain* |
| IQ of a job applicant | About 130 | From 125 to 140 | Exactly 134 |
| Inflation rate for 1994 | About 4% | From 3.5% to 4.5% | Exactly 3.8% |
| Capacity of Airplane (Number of passengers) | About 240 | From 210 to 260 | Exactly 235 |

Zadeh (1965) first introduced the concept of fuzzy set theory to formulate algebraic operations on fuzzy data. The first attempt at applying fuzzy set theory to MADM analysis was done by Bellman and Zadeh (1970). Recently, Chen and Hwang (1992) summarized fuzzy set theory applications in relation to MADM problems. Their book carries a dozen different fuzzy MADM methods. Fuzzy logic has many practical applications but it involves complicated mathematical operations. The uses of fuzzy MADM seem to be limited until efficient algorithms and supporting software are developed.

## 8.2. Decision Support System for MADM

The exponential spread of personal computers has made MADM analyses more accessible to DMs. Many MADM algorithms can be easily executed by a personal computer. A large number of commercial software programs for SAW are available. For example, "Best Choice" is a popular program for AHP. See Hodge, Canada, and Masri (1992) for a MADM software survey. The electronic spreadsheet is an especially powerful tool for MADM analysis. It can store information just as a decision matrix does and is able to manipulate data very easily as required by MADM algorithms. Most solutions in this monograph were obtained by spreadsheets. The utilization of computer graphics in MADM analysis offers yet another opportunity in the computer age. See Korhonen (1988) and Kasanen, Ostermark, and Zeleny (1991) for the current status.

We have encountered a variety of MADM problems and many MADM methods to solve them. Which method should be used to solve a particular problem is itself a MADM problem. There is clearly a need for a Decision

Support System (DSS) that will advise a DM on the proper selection of a MADM method capable of obtaining the best solution for any kind of MADM problem under consideration. Minch and Sanders (1986) presented a general framework on how to build a MADM-DSS. The MADM-DSS built by Hong and Vogel (1991) guides a DM to choose appropriate methods based on the choice strategy. Hwang (1987) created a prototype of a MADM-DSS using an expert system structure. The expert system would be able to extract the problem specifications and data from the DM. It would convert the data if needed. Then it would identify the problem type and a proper solution method. Next it would solve the problem and display the best solution. Despite the enthusiasm to build an efficient MADM-DSS, we wonder if the huge cost of building such a system would be appreciated by MADM users.

### 8.3. Choice and Validity of Methods

Noncompensatory methods usually have a unique decision context that a DM faces, which may make the choice nonarbitrary, but choice among compensatory methods is yet another MADM problem. For instance, a DM could use TOPSIS, ELECTRE, or any one of the scoring methods in the same decision environment. In picking a method, Hobbs, Chakong, Hamadeh, and Stakhiv (1992) suggested keeping the following questions in mind: (a) Which method is appropriate to the problem, the people who will use it, and the institutional setting in which it will be implemented? (b) How easy are the methods to use? (c) Which method is most likely to be valid, that is, to accurately reflect the values of the DMs? (d) Do the results of different methods significantly differ? If the answer to the last question is "yes," then validity becomes crucial.

To answer these questions Hobbs et al. (1992) compared four compensatory methods: SAW, ELECTRE, Minimum Distance From Positive Ideal Solution (which they called goal programming), and MAUT (Multiple Attribute Utility Technique). The subjects of the study were planners from the U.S. Army Corps of Engineers. They found no significant difference in terms of the appropriateness of the method and its ease of use. These results were expected because of the subjects' familiarity with quantitative decision making techniques. Predictive validity can be measured by how well a method predicts unaided decisions made independently of judgments used to fit the model. That is, the alternative ranks resulting from the MADM methods are compared to unaided judgments. In their experiment,

TABLE 8.2

Preference Rankings From Different Methods

| | Methods | | | |
|---|---|---|---|---|
| Applicants | SAW | WP | TOPSIS | ELECTRE |
| A | 5 | 5 | 6 | 4* |
| B | 3 | 4 | 2 | 4* |
| C | 4 | 3 | 4 | 4* |
| D | 2 | 2 | 3 | 2 |
| E | 6 | 6 | 5 | 3 |
| F | 1 | 1 | 1 | 1 |

* indicates tied fourth rank

each DM was asked to state which alternative was most preferred. A method with better predictive validity would result in a high rank for that alternative. They reported a predictive rate of about 68% for ELECTRE and the Displaced Ideal method, whereas other methods had predictive rates that were lower but not significantly so. It is surprising to find that MAUT had poorer predictive ratings than were expected. They concluded that whichever method users feel comfortable with should be used. We may accept their premise if different methods should yield identical preference rankings. The graduate fellowship selection problem (Case 5.1) is considered again to compare the rankings obtained by some MADM methods. Table 8.2 shows rankings obtained by SAW, Weighted Product (WP) method, TOPSIS, and (Complementary) ELECTRE. These rankings are quite stable. Karni, Sanchez, and Tummala (1990) considered three real-life cases to compare rankings by different methods. They found that rankings by AHP, SAW, and ELECTRE do not differ significantly either.

We believe that the choice of a method is not crucial enough for many DMs to be overly concerned about it. Scoring methods are recommended for unsophisticated DMs. For example, the SAW method is popular in evaluating products and services but may be too simple for quantitatively trained DMs. TOPSIS and ELECTRE, on the other hand, are more complex and have been used in federal and local government projects. However, most crucial to a successful MADM analysis is the generation of appropriate attributes. We suggest a goal hierarchy approach to generate attributes and subattributes (Section 2.1). This approach would enable a DM to identify the hierarchy of attributes and avoid comparing and trading off attributes that belong to different levels.

# REFERENCES

ANASTASI, A. (1988) *Psychological Testing*. New York: Macmillan.

BELL, D. E., RAIFFA, H., and TVERSKY, A. (1988) "Descriptive, normative, and prescriptive decision making." In D. E. Bell, H. Raiffa, and A. Tversky (Eds.), *Decision Making: Descriptive, Normative, and Prescriptive Interactions* (pp. 9-30). London: Cambridge University Press.

BELLMAN, R., and ZADEH, L. A. (1970) "Decision making in a fuzzy environment." *Management Science* 17B: 141-164.

BRIDGMAN, P. W. (1922) *Dimensional Analysis*. New Haven, CT: Yale University Press.

CHEN, S. J., and HWANG, C. L. (1992) *Fuzzy Multiple Attribute Decision Making*. Berlin/Heidelberg/New York: Springer-Verlag.

COOK, W. D., and SEIFORD, L. M. (1978) "Priority ranking and consensus formation." *Management Science* 24: 1721-1734.

COOMBS, C. H. (1958) "On the use of inconsistency of preferences in psychological measurement." *Journal of Experimental Psychology* 55: 1-7.

COOMBS, C. H. (1964) *A Theory of Data*. New York: Wiley.

DAWES, R. M. (1964) "Social selection based on multidimensional criteria." *Journal of Abnormal and Social Psychology* 68: 104-109.

DAWES, R. M. (1971) "A case study of graduate admissions: Applications of three principles of human decision making." *American Psychologist* 26: 180-188.

ECKENRODE, R. T. (1965) "Weighting multiple criteria." *Management Science* 12: 180-192.

EDWARDS, W. (1977) "Use of multiattribute utility measurement for social decision making." In D. E. Bell, R. L. Keeney, and H. Raiffa (Eds.), *Conflicting Objectives in Decisions* (pp. 247-276). New York: Wiley.

EDWARDS, W., and NEWMAN, J. R. (1982) *Multiattribute Evaluation*. Sage University Paper series on Quantitative Applications in the Social Sciences, 07-26. Newbury Park, CA: Sage.

FARMER, T. A. (1987) "Testing the robustness of multiattribute utility theory in an applied setting." *Decision Sciences* 18: 178-193.

FISHBURN, P. C. (1976) "Utility independence on subsets of product sets." *Operations Research* 24: 245-255.

HALL, A. D. (1989) *Metasystems Methodology: A New Synthesis and Unification*. Oxford: Pergamon Press.

HOBBS, B. F. (1980) "A comparison of weighting methods in power plant citing." *Decision Sciences* 11: 725-737.

HOBBS, B. F., CHAKONG, V., HAMADEH, W., and STAKHIV, E. Z. (1992) "Does choice of multicriteria method matter? An experiment in water resources planning." *Water Resources Research* 28: 1767-1780.

HODGE, G. L., CANADA, J. R., and MASRI, W. R. (1992) "Low cost software for multi-attribute decision analysis." *The Engineering Economist* 37: 184-191.

HONG, I. B., and VOGEL, D. R. (1991) "Data and model management in a generalized MCDM-DDS." *Decision Sciences* 22: 1-25.

HWANG, C.L., LAI, Y. J., and LIU, T. Y. (1993) "A new approach for multiple objective decision making." *Computers and Operation Research* 20: 889-899.

HWANG, C. L., and MASUD, A. S. M. with PAIDY, S. R., and YOON, K. (1979) *Multiple Objective Decision Making: Methods and Applications.* Berlin/Heidelberg/ New York: Springer-Verlag.

HWANG, C. L., and YOON, K. (1981) *Multiple Attribute Decision Making: Methods and Applications.* Berlin/Heidelberg/New York: Springer-Verlag.

HWANG, C. L. and LIN, M.J. (1987) *Group Decision Making Under Multiple Criteria: Methods and Applications.* Berlin/Heidelberg/New York: Springer-Verlag.

HWANG, F. P. (1987) *An Expert Decision Making Support System for Multiple Attribute Decision Making.* Unpublished doctoral dissertation, Kansas State University.

KARNI, R., SANCHEZ, P., and TUMMALA, V. M. R. (1990) "A comparative study of multiattribute decision making methodologies." *Theory and Decision* 29: 203-222.

KASANEN, E., OSTERMARK, R., and ZELENY, M. (1991) "Gestalt system of holistic graphics: New management support view of MCDM." *Computers and Operations Research* 18: 233-239.

KEENEY, R. L., and RAIFFA, H. (1976) *Decisions With Multiple Objectives.* New York: Wiley.

KORHONEN, P. (1988) "A visual reference direction approach to solving discrete multiple criteria problems." *European Journal of Operational Research* 34: 152-159.

KUHN, H. W. (1955) "The Hungarian method for the assignment problem." *Naval Research Logistics Quarterly* 2: 83-85.

LOUVIERE, J. J. (1988) *Analyzing Decision Making: Metric Conjoint Analysis.* Sage University Paper series on Quantitative Applications in the Social Sciences, 07-67. Newbury Park, CA: Sage.

LUCE, R. D. (1956) "Semiorders and a theory of utility discrimination." *Econometrica* 24: 178-191.

LYNCH, J. G. (1985) "Uniqueness issues in the decompositional modeling of multiattribute overall evaluations." *Journal of Marketing Research* 22: 1-19.

MacCRIMMON, K. R. (1968) *Decision Making Among Multiple-Attribute Alternatives: A Survey and Consolidated Approach.* RAND Memorandum RM-4823-ARPA.

MacCRIMMON, K. R. (1973) "An overview of multiple objective decision making." In J. L. Cochrane and M. Zeleny (Eds.), *Multiple Criteria Decision Making* (pp. 18-43). Columbia, SC: University of South Carolina Press.

McANARNEY, D. K. (1987) *Multiple Attribute Decision Making Methods: A Comparative Study.* Unpublished master's thesis, Kansas State University.

McIVER, J. P., and CARMINES, E. G. (1981) *Unidimensional Scaling.* Sage University Paper series in Quantitative Applications in the Social Sciences, 07-24. Newbury Park, CA: Sage.

MILLER, G. A. (1956) "The magic number seven, plus or minus two." *Psychological Review* 63: 81-97.

MINCH, R. P., and SANDERS, G. L. (1986) "Computerized information systems supporting multicriteria decision making." *Decision Sciences* 17: 395-413.

MORRIS, W. T. (1964) *The Analysis of Management Decisions.* Homewood, IL: Irwin.

NAGASHIMA, K. (1986) *Inference System for Selection of an Appropriate Multiple Attribute Decision Making Method.* Unpublished master's thesis, Kansas State University.

72

NIJKAMP P., and VAN DELFT, A. (1977) *Multi-Criteria Analysis and Regional Decision Making.* Leiden, The Netherlands: Martinus Nijhoff.

OSGOOD, C. E., SUCI, G. J., and TANNENBAUM, P. H. (1975) *The Measurement of Meaning.* Urbana, IL: The University of Illinois Press.

PARDEE, E. S. (1969) *Measurement and Evaluation of Transportation System Effectiveness.* RAND Memorandum RM-5869-DOT.

PATON, R. F., and BRADBURY, P. L. (1987) *Host State Recommendation for Central Interstate Compact Commission's Waste Management Facility.* Louisville, KY: US Ecology/Bechtel, Inc.

PUGH, E. M., and WINSLOW, G. W. (1966) *The Analysis of Physical Measurement.* Reading, MA: Addison-Wesley.

ROY, B. (1971) "Problems and methods with multiple objective functions." *Mathematical Programming* 1: 239-266.

SAATY, T. L. (1980) *The Analytical Hierarchial Process.* New York: Wiley.

SAATY, T. L., VARGAS, L. G., and BARZILAY, A. (1982) "High-level decisions: A lesson from the Iran hostage rescue operation." *Decision Sciences* 13: 185-206.

SIMON, H. A. (1957) *Models of Man.* New York: Wiley.

SOUDER, W. E. (1978) "A system for using R&D project evaluation methods." *Research Management* 21: 29-37.

SPECTOR, P. E. (1992) *Summated Rating Scale Construction: An Introduction.* Sage University Paper Series on Quantitative Applications in the Social Sciences, 07-82. Thousand Oaks, CA: Sage.

STARR, M. K. (1972) *Production Management.* Englewood Cliffs, NJ: Prentice-Hall.

STILLWELL, W. G., SEAVER, D. A., and EDWARDS, W. (1981) "A comparison of weight approximation techniques in multiattribute utility decision making." *Organizational Behavior and Human Performance* 28: 62-77.

SWENSON, P. A., and McCAHON, C. S. (1991) "A MADM justification of a budget reduction decision." *OMEGA* 19: 539-548.

TVERSKY, A. (1969) "Intransitivity of preferences." *Psychological Review* 76: 31-48.

TVERSKY, A. (1972) "Elimination by aspects: A theory of choice." *Psychological Review* 79: 281-299.

TVERSKY, A., and KAHNEMAN, D. (1974) "Judgements under uncertainty: Heuristics and biases." *Science* 185: 1124-1131.

TVERSKY, A., and KAHNEMAN, D. (1981) "The framing of decisions and the psychology of choice." *Science* 211: 453-458.

VOOGD, H. (1983) *Multicriteria Evaluation for Urban and Regional Planning.* London: Pion.

YOON, K. (1987) "A reconciliation among discrete compromise situations." *Journal of Operational Research Society* 38: 277-286.

YOON, K. (1989) "The propagation of errors in multiple-attribute decision analysis: A practical approach." *Journal of Operational Research Society* 40: 681-686.

YOON, K. (1990) "Capital investment analysis involving estimate error." *The Engineering Economist* 36: 21-30.

YOON, K., and HWANG, C. L. (1985) "Manufacturing plant location analysis by multiple attribute decision making." *International Journal of Production Research* 23: 345-359.

YOON, K., and KIM, G. (1989) "Multiple attribute decision analysis with imprecise information." *IIE Transactions* 21: 21-26.

YU, P. L (1985) *Multiple Criteria Decision Making: Concepts, Techniques and Extensions.* New York: Plenum.

ZADEH, L. A. (1965) "Fuzzy sets." *Information and Control* 8: 338-353.

ZAHEDI, F. (1986) "The analytic hierarchy process—A survey of the method and its applications." *Interfaces* 16: 96-108.

ZELENY, M. (1982) *Multiple Criteria Decision Making.* New York: McGraw-Hill.

# ABOUT THE AUTHORS

*K. PAUL YOON* is Professor of Information Systems and Sciences at Fairleigh Dickinson University. He has taught quantitative methods and operations management. His B.S. degree is from Seoul National University, Korea, and his M.S. and Ph.D. degrees are from Kansas State University. His research areas include multiple criteria decision analysis and its applications to service and production systems. He is the coauthor (with Hwang) of two books on multiple criteria decision making.

*CHING-LAI HWANG* is Professor of Industrial Engineering at Kansas State University. His major research interests are systems engineering and optimization, multiple criteria decision making, and fuzzy sets theory and applications. He received his B.S. from National Taiwan University and his M.S. and Ph.D. from Kansas State University. In addition to about 150 professional journal articles, he is the coauthor of the books *Optimization of Systems Reliability* (1980), *Multiple Objective Decision Making* (with Yoon et al., 1979), *Multiple Attribute Decision Making* (with Yoon, 1981), *Group Decision Making Under Multiple Criteria* (1987), *Fuzzy Multiple Attribute Decision Making* (1992), *Fuzzy Mathematical Programming* (1992), and *Fuzzy Multiple Objective Decision Making* (1994).